This book is due for return on or before the last date shown below.

Published in 2015 by Hardie Grant Books

Hardie Grant Books (Australia)
Ground Floor, Building 1
658 Church Street
Richmond, Victoria 3121
www.hardiegrant.com.au

Hardie Grant Books (UK)
5th & 6th Floors
52–54 Southwark Street
London SE1 1UN
www.hardiegrant.co.uk

Cataloguing in publications data available from the National Library of Australia
Those Summers of Cricket: Richie Benaud
ISBN 9781 74379097 7

Publisher: Pam Brewster
Cover design: Luke Causby, Blue Cork
Internal design: Peter Daniel

Colour reproduction by Splitting Image Colour Studio
Printed and bound in China by 1010 Printing International Limited

THOSE SUMMERS OF CRICKET
RICHIE BENAUD
1930-2015

hardie grant books

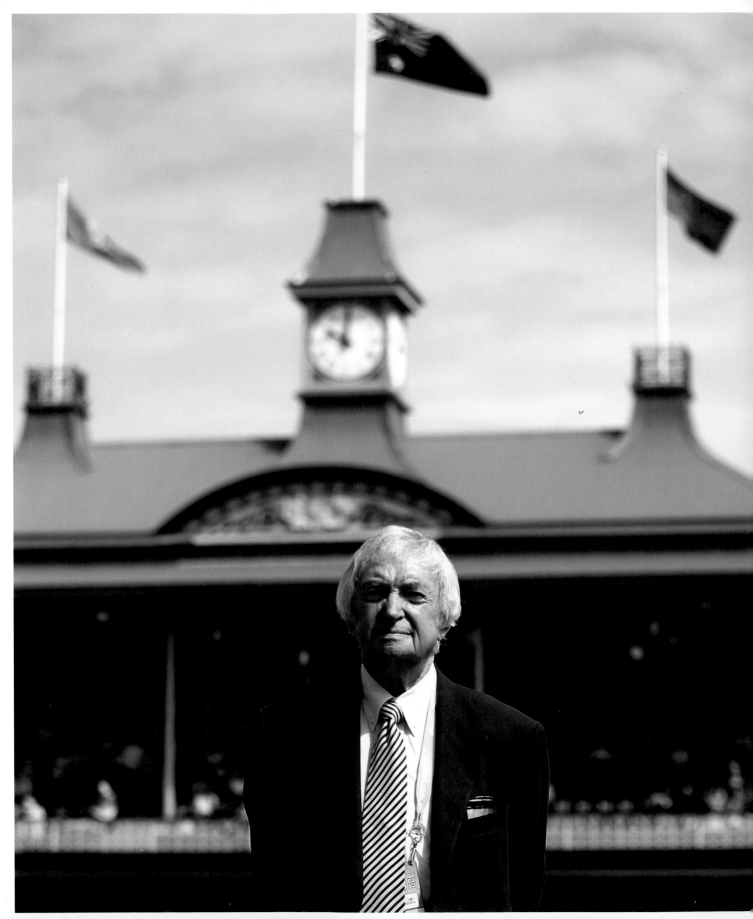

CONTENTS

EARLY YEARS

Jugiong in the 1930s. (State Records NSW)

JOHN BENAUD

from *Matters of Choice*

There was no doctor at Koorawatha in 1930 and [our mother] Rene had to travel back to Penrith, [our father] Lou's home town, to have Rich. He was premature, and sickly, and the doctor forbade Rene to take him back to Koorawatha.

After six weeks there was only slight improvement in his condition, but the doctor relented. Rene, with Rich, and supported by Lou's sister, made the long journey home by steam train, a heatwave all the way, and dusty.

When school broke up for the summer holidays, Lou and Rene brought Rich back to Penrith and took him to the doctor for a check-up.

Rene remembers the moment, the doctor talking to Lou: 'I'll tell you now Lou, I let that little fellow go home to die. He must have wanted to live. I could do nothing more for him.'

Lou wrote: 'At Jugiong public school, when Rich was about four, a very small bat was cut from packing case timber and he began to hit a tennis ball with the bat.

'The school residence was a huge place because one of the teachers, who had lived there some years before we did, had a very large family so some extra rooms had to be built on to the original residence.

'We did not use any of those extra rooms as living quarters, but as Richie progressed in his cricket skills, one of the empty rooms was used by him when he played with the bat and ball.

'In addition to having a bat and ball he also had a pencil and scorebook. He wrote down (the names of) two Test sides and he became batsman, bowler, fieldsman, wicketkeeper, umpire and scorer.

'Maybe he was a little patriotic, for Australia won more Tests than the other sides. It was sweet music to hear the ball being hit in that room for it signified that Rich had developed a keenness for cricket.

'Towards the end of our stay at Jugiong, Rich had his first game of cricket against a team from Bookham Public School. He was only six years old and to a parent, doting or otherwise, it was a rather frightening experience to see the little chap facing up to a fast, lifting compo ball (compressed cork), bowled by lads nearly twice his size, on coir mat.'

SCHOOLBOYS PLAYING CRICKET. (NLA)

STEVE CANNANE

from *First Tests: Great Australian cricketers and the backyards that made them*

In his later years as a commentator, Richie Benaud had an audience in the millions. But at the beginning of his cricketing life, in the isolated country town of Jugiong, he had only himself to entertain. His father Lou was the sole teacher at Jugiong Public School between 1932 and 1937. The school, about 350km south-west of Sydney, had 23 students of various ages.

After school, there were no kids around to share Richie's passion for cricket. His father came to the rescue, giving him a home-made bat and a tennis ball, and clearing out an old storeroom attached to the school. As a Test cricketer Richie played aggressively. He scored his runs fast, bowled probing leg-spin and was renowned as an attacking captain. But there, on his own, with his little cut-down bat made from packing-case timber, young Richie started off by playing two shots, the forward defence and the back foot defence.

For most kids, slogging across the line is all they want to do when they first pick up a bat. So what was a young boy on the banks of the Murrumbidgee doing blocking a tennis ball against a wall? It sounds more like the formative years of Geoffrey Boycott or Trevor Bailey, not a man who would go on to score one of Test cricket's fastest centuries.

Lou Benaud knew exactly what he was doing. If Richie was to learn how to bat, he had to start with the basics. Lou was a top-class cricketer who'd been denied the opportunity to push for state selection. In 1925, the Department of Education shipped him off to One Tree Farm Provisional School, about 1000km north of Sydney. He spent the next 12 years teaching at various country schools. At least three times he had to turn down the chance to trial before state selectors. The latter part of his country stint coincided with the Great Depression, so Lou didn't have much choice; he had to hold on to his job and accept his lot.

In that storeroom at Jugiong, young Richie learned more than just defensive shots. Soon he progressed to playing 'test' matches against the wall. Like Bradman against the tank stand in Bowral, he picked an English XI and an Australian XI, set an imaginary field and threw the ball against the wall, hitting it off the rebound. Just like Bowral, the pitch was undercover, maximising game time during wet weather. The enclosed walls meant he didn't have to spend valuable time chasing balls.

Whereas Bradman used a golf ball and a stump, Benaud used a tennis ball and cut-off bat. For a boy of five or six it was perfect training. As Benaud wrote in *On Reflection*, 'Coming from only 15 feet and bouncing, it could be a reasonably difficult assignment. It certainly improved my eye!'

Richie played for hours in the storeroom. Although he'd never seen a Test match, he imagined he was playing for Australia. The thud of the tennis ball hitting repetitively against the walls filtered back into the school residence. It was sweet music to hear the ball being hit in that room, Lou remembered, for it signified that Richie had developed a keenness for cricket.

When Richie was seven, the Benaud family moved back to Sydney. Lou had scored a job at Burnside Public School, North Parramatta. The family took up residence 1km from the school at 5 Sutherland Road. Richie's younger brother, John, who also played Test cricket, was not born until Richie was 13, so he continued to play his one-man tests, this time against a brick wall on the back veranda. Rene Benaud kept a beautiful garden, but that didn't mean her son had to modify his range of strokes. 'My mother grew to understand that the really important thing was that I'd made 29 playing against England this day, and if there was a pot plant or two that had to be renovated that was OK,' Richie recalls.

His veranda test matches were taken very seriously. He wrote the scores in his *Unrivalled Pocket Cricket Scoring Book*. Once full, he rubbed them out and started again. Unsurprisingly he called these games as if he was part of the ABC Radio commentary team.

In January 1940, Richie saw his first game of first-class cricket. Aged nine, his father took him by bus, steam train and tram to the SCG to watch NSW play

Father Benaud, who reminds many of Father Hoad, Lew Hoad's dad, took 10 wickets in an innings as a spin bowler for Cumberland Cricket Club out by the River Parramatta that flows 'tidal with eternity', as Ernest Raymond called it, into Sydney Harbour. Raymond, of course, was writing of the Thames, comparing it with the Fal that rushes like some young Graeme Pollock in search of a century towards Falmouth.

Father Benaud was not upset, quite the contrary, when his elder son Richie dislodged him from the Cumberland team. He just loved it and retired gracefully and contentedly to the new Benaud homestead at the foot of the beautiful Blue Mountains.

— R.S. WHITINGTON FROM
BRADMAN, BENAUD AND GODDARD'S CINDERELLAS

BURNSIDE WINS CRICKET CHAMPIONSHIP:

Burnside schoolboys, defeated Guildford in the grand final of the Parramatta District Cricket Championship. Guildford was dismissed for 33 and 68. Billiingham and Benaud took six wickets each. Burnside scored 200 (Burns 55, Barnes 42, Benaud 37, Lindsay 26). In this competition, Richie Benaud scored 415 runs and was dismissed only once.

— The Cumberland Argus and Fruitgrowers Advocate,
26 November 1941

STOP PRESS

Sydney: Richie Benaud, 16-year-old Cumberland first grader, took eight wickets for 11 for Metropolitan High Schools against Northern High Schools at Chatswood Oval today.

— The Newcastle Sun, 10 December 1946

JUNIOR SOCCER

Results of last week's Granville District Football.

Under 18 A Div.: Parramatta Meths 10: (R. Benaud 9, J. Ashwood), Mascot Congs. 0. Richie Benaud was in top form to notch 9 goals, bringing his season's number of goals scored to 46.

— The Cumberland Argus and Fruitgrowers Advocate,
30 July 1947

South Australia. Over 30,000 came to what was one of the last Sheffield Shield matches before the war intervened. It was so crowded that Richie sat in the aisle with his dad in the old Sheridan Stand. Leg-spinner Clarrie Grimmett dominated, taking 6–118.

Richie could not have had a better mentor than his father. He was there for him at every stage, from crafting him a bat at Jugiong to coaching him in the intricacies of leg-spin in his teen years. Lou instilled in Richie that there was a right way to play cricket. 'Cricket was talked breakfast, lunch and dinner in the Benaud household, every day I can remember,' Richie recalls. 'It was drilled into me over meal tables at home when I was a child that cricketers who do not set about trying to win the game from the start of the match would never be successful, but don't forget the game must be played in the right spirit.' It was this attitude that Benaud carried through into his captaincy of the Australian side. In the 1960s, he helped revive international cricket with positive, aggressive play, at a time when Test matches had become bogged down in negative tactics and meaningless draws.

Lou also encouraged his son to practise and play the game whenever he could. When Richie wasn't playing his veranda test matches he would join boys in the neighbourhood for a game in the paddock across the road. The boys built a dirt pitch by digging out the grass and levelling it with a shovel. They watered the pitch and occasionally flattened it out with a roller borrowed from a nearby tennis court.

RICHIE BENAUD PREPARES TO BAT. (FAIRFAX)

HOW TO PLAY CRICKET

AIM: To endeavour to play cricket.

APPARATUS:

1. A lump of wood shaped at one end to represent a handle.

2. A piece of round rubber, preferably without edges.

3. A plot of grass, about 5 acres in radius, having as its centre a rectangle 22 yards by 8 yards, with a ditch in the centre (if you are a bowler).

4. Six pieces of wood for stumps (the bigger they are the harder they fall).

5. Eleven fieldsmen.

6. Batsman and two umpires.

METHOD: The bowler walks or waddles, to the bowling crease, delivers the ball, and endeavours to hit the stumps. The batsman, taking his stance at the wicket, endeavours to hit the ball. To the fieldsmen falls the honour of chasing the ball.

RESULTS: The ditch in the centre of the wicket is responsible for the injuries, which invariably happen (most of our first grade bowlers get their wickets by means of the ditch). Also if the batsman swipes too hard, he is liable to asphyxiate silly, silly point.

CONCLUSION: From the article you will see that skittles would be easier.

— R. BENAUD, 1944 PARRAMATTA HIGH SCHOOL MAGAZINE

DON BRADMAN PLAYS A COVER DRIVE AT THE SYDNEY
CRICKET GROUND. (SAM HOOD, SLNSW)

My father was an outstanding country cricketer and then a very good first-grade player when he moved to Central Cumberland [now Parramatta] in the Sydney competition. He was also a splendid coach who guided his two sons, John and me, to play for Australia. In addition, he was a very good tactician and his advice was always valuable.

'My father took me to the SCG for the first time when NSW were playing South Australia on January 13, 1940. Bradman and Stan McCabe were the captains, the crowd on the first day was 30,400 and, aged nine, I watched [Clarrie] Grimmett take six for 118. We went home to Parramatta, and early next morning I was trying to bowl leg-breaks against the wall at the back of the house.'

— JOHN BUCHANAN, FROM *LEARNING FROM LEGENDS*

Lou also encouraged his son to practise and play the game whenever he could. After the Benauds came back to Sydney, Lou was drafted back into Cumberland's first-grade side. This introduced Richie to the world of men's cricket at a young age. 'I was able to go to the Tuesday and the Thursday practices and I was allowed to field and it taught me not to fear the cricket ball. It came pretty fast.' The lack of fear was to become an important ingredient in Richie's make-up as a cricketer. He was a courageous hooker of fast bowling and nerveless close-in fielder. At 19, he lost a year of cricket after he shattered the frontal bone in his forehead while trying to hook Victorian quick Jack Daniel.

— STEVE CANNANE FROM *FIRST TESTS: GREAT AUSTRALIAN CRICKETERS AND THE BACKYARDS THAT MADE THEM*

A CLOSE-UP TAKEN IN THE 1940S OF A SPIN BOWLER'S GRIP.
(SAM HOOD, SLNSW)

CRICKETER

JOHN BENAUD

from *Matters of Choice*

I have this mind picture … I was the smallest of boys, only four years old, trailing close behind Rene as she walked down the hallway of our North Parramatta home to answer a loud knock at the front door.

Rene opened the door, and I can still hear her urgent gasp, 'Oh, Rich …' I looked up and saw Rich; his usually cricket-tanned face was black and yellow in colour. This is what had happened, related later by Lou:

'In a Second XI match at Melbourne in the 1948–49 season, Rich tried to hook a bumper but he was hit on the forehead. He was taken to hospital and x-rayed. The x-ray was negative. When he returned home we were deeply shocked by the extremely bruised and swollen appearance of his face.

'He went to see Dr Jack Jeffery, a great lover of cricket, and further x-rays were taken. The doctor called at our place the following Saturday morning and asked where Richie was. We told him that Rich had gone to Lidcombe Oval to watch Cumberland first grade play a match.'

'The doctor gave us a severe shock when he informed us that Rich had a severely shattered frontal bone in his head and then he asked us to ring the oval and tell Richie not to practise in the nets as a blow on the injured head would result in his death. After a successful operation Rich was able to play cricket again during the next cricket season.'

Later in his career, Rich wrote about this incident, and did so advisedly:

'One of the most exciting sights in cricket is a fast bowler being belted by a good hooker … I still like to go for the hook myself, although it once nearly put paid to my career when I was playing for the NSW Second XI. I got right behind the line of a bumper from Victoria's Jack Daniel, missed it and was taken to hospital with a fractured skull.'

You see, the bumper is one ball you must not get behind. Instead you must go further across. You need to move right inside the line of flight and that means moving quickly enough so that your body is across to the off-side and the ball is passing down the leg-side, then forget all about playing the hook. It will either get you out, or injured.

RICHIE BENAUD SHOWS
HIS BATTING STYLE. (AAP)

JOHN BUCHANAN

from *Learning from Legends*

Richie might not have considered himself, or anyone, a completely natural leader, but he always seemed to find himself in positions of leadership. 'I captained the Burnside Public School team at North Parramatta in 1940 and 1941, then the Parramatta High School fourth-grade team and later the first-grade team, so I had some valuable early experience of leadership. In 1946, Parramatta High won the first-grade premiership, as they had done when my father played for them in 1924.'

Richie was first selected for NSW in 1948, aged just 18. 'Listen and watch! Listen and remember! When I first played at the SCG in the NSW Sheffield Shield team on December 31, 1948, it was under Arthur Morris's captaincy and with other Test players in the team. Jim Burke and I had played in the NSW Colts team in Brisbane a few weeks earlier, and the selectors were looking for promising young players. Jim made 29 not out in our second innings, opening with Morris, who made 108 not out in 82 minutes in the winning total of 0–143. I knew I was out of my class at that time, but I was even more determined to listen and watch and remember and learn.

'I was very lucky to be in the NSW team and then the Australian team with Arthur Morris, Keith Miller and Ray Lindwall. They were wonderful with all the young players, brilliant at noticing where we might have gone wrong with some part of the bowling, batting or fielding. They were then constructive with their advice. Three of the greatest.'

Richie paid attention, doing enough watching, listening and learning to make the Test team three years later. However, he initially struggled to make much of an impact. The selectors saw enough to persevere with him over the next six years, but it wasn't until his outstanding series with both bat and ball in South Africa in 1957–58 that Richie fully repaid their faith. And from there he went from strength to strength. Appointed Test captain later in 1958 in the absence of the ill Ian Craig and ahead of the more experienced and better-performed Neil Harvey, Richie led the team to a 4–0 victory over England and Australia regained the Ashes for the first time since 1950–51.

New South Wales batsman, Richie Benaud, escapes being stumped during a Sheffield Shield match against Queensland at the Gabba, Brisbane, in November 1953. (Bob Millar Jnr/Newspix)

BENAUD'S BIG WEEKEND

All-rounder Richie Benaud has his 21st birthday today, and he hopes to celebrate it with further success for his club, Central Cumberland. On top of that, he wants to have his name included in the season's first state team, to be chosen on Monday.

— SYDNEY MORNING HERALD, 6 OCTOBER 1951

100 BY BENAUD

A fine century by Richie Benaud saved New South Wales in their first innings against South Australia yesterday. Benaud and Kissell put on 76 for the sixth wicket in 61 minutes. Their partnership enabled New South Wales to extricate themselves from a serious position, and lead South Australia on the first innings. Kissell was out for 35, but Benaud went on to 100 not out.

Benaud batted brilliantly, and hit with power in front of the wicket. He took 90 minutes to get his 50, and hit seven fours. His 100 came in 164 minutes, including 11 fours and one six.

— DAILY MERCURY, 3 DECEMBER 1951

HIGHLIGHTS OF YESTERDAY'S PLAY WERE:

Richie Benaud's unconquered innings of 167 runs – his highest score in a first-class match.

Benaud's seventh-wicket stand with left-hander Alan Davidson, which yielded 167 runs in 86 minutes, and 143 in the first hour after the luncheon adjournment.

Benaud's only first-class century prior to yesterday was 117 for NSW against South Australia in a Sheffield Shield match on Adelaide Oval in the 1951–52 season. Grim determination and sound technical defence characterised Benaud's innings of 187 minutes yesterday.

A delightfully executed square cut past point off Neil Harvey posted Benaud's 50 (nine 4s) in 72 minutes. Davidson, his partner, had reached the half century 13 minutes faster and his century went up in 132 after he had gently steered Cowley to backward point and taken a single. It included 15 boundaries. When Australia's first innings ended for 469 at 5.20pm, Benaud remained unconquered for 167. He had batted 187 minutes and his chanceless innings was studded with three sixes and 21 fours.

— EXAMINER, 14 MARCH 1953

FAST CENTURY BY RICHIE BENAUD

New South Wales all-rounder Richie Benaud scored the fastest century in a first-class match in Perth since the war for the Australian XI against Western Australia today. Benaud completely overshadowed his batting partner, Ian Craig, to score 100 not out in 106 minutes.

— THE MERCURY, 21 MARCH 1953

MAILEY COACHES BENAUD

The former international slow bowler, Arthur Mailey, believes that 22-year-old all-rounder Richie Benaud, will be Australia's outstanding spin bowler on the forthcoming tour of England. Mailey, who is travelling with the team, said today; 'Apart from Fleetwood Smith Benaud spins the ball more than any other slow bowler I have seen in the last 20 years. He is strong, keen and had the pace necessary to reap a harvest of wickets in England provided he is given plenty of work.'

— MARYBOROUGH CHRONICLE, 13 APRIL 1953

RICHIE BENAUD IS TEAM STAR

Richie Benaud was the star at the Australians' only cricket practice last week. He surprised the English critics by spinning the ball viciously. He had appeared innocuous to them when they toured Australia with Freddie Brown's team. Australia badly needs a successful leg-break bowler. Benaud could fill the position.

— THE ADVOCATE, 20 APRIL 1953

The Australia cricket team: (back row, left to right) scorer and baggage master N. Gorman, Ian Craig, Ken MacKay, Jim Burke, Pat Crawford, Peter Burge, Laurie Maddocks, Jack Rutherford, Jack Wilson, unknown; (front row, left to right) team manager W.H. Dowling, Ron Archer, Gil Langley, Ray Lindwall, Ian Johnson, Keith Miller, Neil Harvey, Richie Benaud, Colin McDonald. (AAP Images)

RICHIE BENAUD AS BATSMAN AND BOWLER

Richie Benaud showed superlative form in the match against Yorkshire, making 97 runs. He hit four great sixers and a number of fours. Cricket lovers sympathised with him for missing his century, and he just failed by six runs to get a century before lunch. At the same time Keith Miller went along to 159 not out, and at lunch Morris closed the innings at six wickets for 453.

— Border Watch, 9 May 1953

RICHIE BENAUD

English cricket writers shared some of the dismay which shocked the Bradford crowd into silence when Ray Lindwall bowled Len Hutton for a duck yesterday. However, they were not stinting in their praise for Richie Benaud's double – his fine 97 and seven cheap wickets in Yorkshire's first innings. Alex Bannister, of the London *Daily Mail*, said: 'If Benaud's batting carried the hallmark of class, his leg-break bowling was equally impressive. He attacks the stumps, keeps a good length and really spins the ball.'

The *Daily Mirror* writer said: 'Benaud flighted the ball well and fully deserved his seven for 46, but otherwise there was nothing in the Australian attack to warrant Yorkshire's batting paralysis.'

The cricket-writer of the *Daily Telegraph* wrote: 'What more could be asked of any all-rounder? This was a wonderful day's work in any company.'

The *Daily Sketch* said: 'Lindwall's astounding guided missile started Yorkshire on the road to disaster. Then came a string of batsmen who shaped as nervously as men entering a dentist's surgery. One by one they went out to the excellent spin bowling of Benaud.'

The Times commented: 'The ball that bowled Hutton was more than an event. It was a calamity for the proud north, and evoked as telling a silence as one can remember.'

Charles Bray, of the *Daily Herald* said: 'They know their cricket in Yorkshire, and 20,000 good folk gave the tall, fair-haired young Australian a reception he is not likely to forget. I doubt if even Miller hit the ball harder or better, and his bowling was in keeping with his batting.'

— The West Australian, 9 May 1953

BENAUD AS SAVIOUR

Richie Benaud, who scored 70 in 86 minutes, saved the Australians from embarrassment when they began a three-day match against Derbyshire at Chesterfield today. At stumps Australia had lost 9 for 191. Half the Australian side was out for 89 when Benaud joined Craig. Benaud, in an onslaught against bowlers, including a new-ball attack, hit up 68 of the 85 run sixth-wicket partnership.

— NORTHERN MINER CHARTERS TOWERS, 18 JUNE 1953

BENAUD, CORNOCK, ACHIEVED 'DOUBLE'

Cumberland all-rounders, Richie Benaud and Walter Cornock, achieved a notable double during the 1952–53 season. Both players gained their 1000 runs and 100 wickets in first grade for the club.

Benaud, now in England with the Test team, headed the batting averages with 49 from an aggregate of 196. He secured 11 wickets for an average of 38.4. By a strange coincidence his father, Lou Benaud, headed the second-grade batting average, with 49 from an aggregate of 196.

— THE CUMBERLAND ARGUS, 29 JULY 1953

BENAUD BRISBANE IDOL

Twenty-three-year-old NSW and Test all-rounder Richie Benaud became the idol of the Brisbane crowd today with a magnificent 158 runs. The crowd today gave a hand to the younger Benaud, some of whose vicious driving went straight through the fieldsmen. Benaud received a roaring ovation when he lost his wicket. He took 179 minutes for his 150, which included 23 fours. Morris was 149 when Benaud reached his 150. The last 50 by the pair had taken only 25 minutes, mainly due to Benaud's aggression, which brought him two successive fours.

— THE MAIL, 14 NOVEMBER 1953

BENAUD BRILLIANT

Richie Benaud starred in a NSW recovery against Western Australia at the Sydney Cricket Ground today when he slammed a brilliant century in 157 minutes. His innings included 19 fours. Benaud went from 59 to 109 in 20 minutes. He hit with tremendous power and once hit six fours in succession.

— THE NEWS, 8 FEBRUARY 1954

BENAUD'S DOUBLE

All-rounder Richie Benaud has scored the most runs and taken the most wickets this season for NSW in Sheffield Shield matches. Benaud scored 665 runs at an average of more than 60 an innings and took 30 wickets at 27.7 runs. The next highest scoring batsmen were Keith Miller, Ron Briggs, Arthur Morris and Jim de Courcy – all with averages exceeding 50.

— THE COURIER MAIL, 25 FEBRUARY 1954

RICHIE COULD OPEN IN TEST

Sydneysider Richie Benaud could come into calculations as Test opener if there is any trouble in finding a partner for Arthur Morris this season, although he has no aspirations in this regard.

Benaud has been opening for his club, Cumberland, in the Sydney competition and has been the most successful opener of the season there. He scored a dashing 140 against Waverley last Saturday, and after four trips to the wicket for once not out, he had knocked up 338 runs at an average of just on 113. Included in his aggregate are two centuries. Benaud is taking wickets as well as getting runs, so his place in the Test side is not in doubt, and he could prove doubly valuable as an opener.

— SPORTING GLOBE, 13 OCTOBER 1954

[KEITH] MILLER FEARS DULL TESTS

While Australian XI batsmen were busy licking their wounds after Saturday's play against the Englishmen, spectators were wending their way home from the MCG muttering to themselves over the dreary day's cricket.

That has been the theme song for spectators for some seasons now, and they are getting tired of it. From the two days' play I saw I formed the opinion that we were in for another season of dull cricket.

On Friday, while Ian Johnson and Richie Benaud tantalisingly threw the ball high into the air, the English batsmen – with the exception of Simpson and Compton, anchored one foot behind the batting crease, and pushed the left foot nervously forward as though seeking a path through a thick minefield, and played a dead bat.

— THE NEWS, 8 NOVEMBER 1954

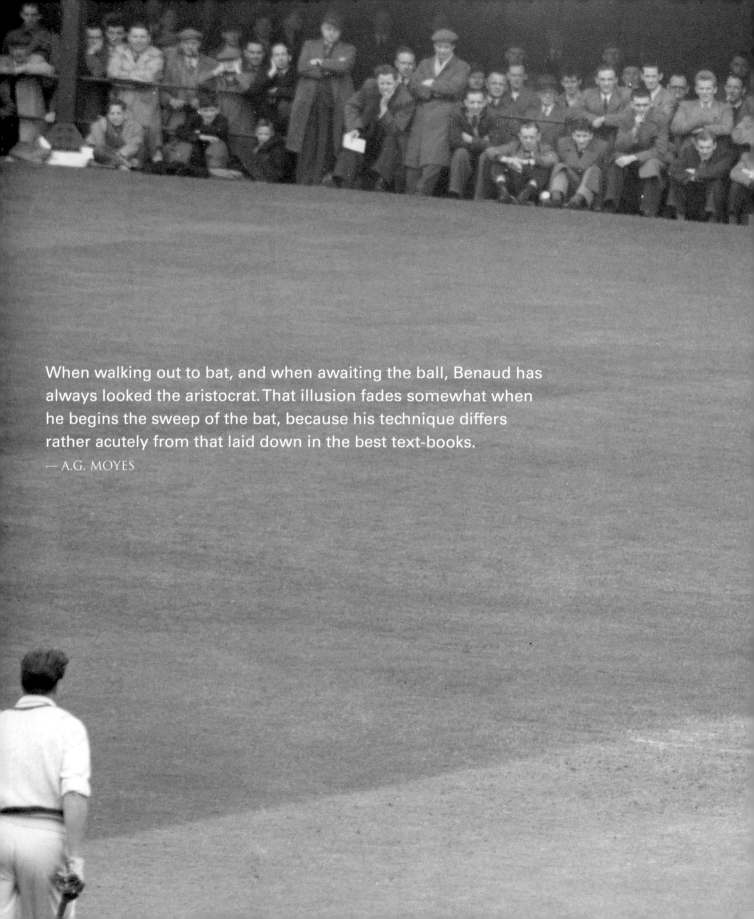

When walking out to bat, and when awaiting the ball, Benaud has always looked the aristocrat. That illusion fades somewhat when he begins the sweep of the bat, because his technique differs rather acutely from that laid down in the best text-books.

— A.G. MOYES

RICHIE BENAUD HITS A BALL FOR SIX FROM NORMAN
YARDLEY IN HIS INNINGS FOR AUSTRALIA AGAINST
YORKSHIRE AT BRADFORD IN ENGLAND. (AAP IMAGES)

TEST TEAM NEEDS DRASTIC OVERHAUL

Australia's selectors should discard Arthur Morris and Graeme Hole from the team for the fourth Test. Other members of the beaten third Test team whose claims must be reviewed are Les Favell, Richie Benaud and Ian Johnson … Benaud has not realised his possibilities in Test cricket. He has a lot of ability but his general form here certainly does not ensure his retention.

— SYDNEY MORNING HERALD, 6 JANUARY 1955

ANXIETY SPURS

Just before Richie Benaud went out to hit his 121 in 96 minutes against the West Indies today [in Kingston, Jamaica], he received word to say his wife was ill, and had been taken to hospital. When captain Ian Johnson joined Benaud a few minutes later Benaud walked up the pitch and spoke to Johnson.

Said Benaud: 'I just heard my wife is ill and gone to hospital. I can't concentrate.'

Replied Johnson: 'Well, just let your head go and hit.'

Benaud … hit and drove his way to the fastest Test century in 52 years.

— THE ARGUS, 17 JUNE 1955

RECORDS TUMBLE IN AUSTRALIA'S TEST INNINGS

Australia yesterday ran up the highest score in the history of Test cricket. As a result, the West Indies' 357 and 1-60 against Australia's 8-758 declared, requires 341 runs to avert an innings defeat. But with the pitch taking spin, Australia should win well inside the final two days of play. Australia's performances have not only placed it in an unbeatable position, but have proved a statistician's dream. These are the records which Australia so far has set in this game:

- A total of 8–758 declared, beats the previous biggest Test score of 6–729 declared against England at Lord's in 1930.
- Five centuries, beats the record of four centuries in one innings by England against Australia at Trent Bridge in 1938
- First Test match centuries by Archer and Benaud

In Richie Benaud's first Test century, raised in 78 minutes, he hit 15 fours and two sixers. At one stage he hit the new ball for 48 runs in three overs.

— THE CANBERRA TIMES, 17 JUNE 1955

AUSTRALIA BATSMAN, RICHIE BENAUD, IS CAUGHT BY GODFREY
EVANS OFF THE BOWLING OF ALEC BEDSER FOR 47 RUNS IN THE
THIRD TEST OF THE AUSTRALIA V ENGLAND SERIES OF 1954–1955
IN MELBOURNE. (GETTY IMAGES)

JOHN BENAUD

from *Matters of Choice*

Rich was one of three cricketers the selectors chose for a Test debut against the West Indies in the 1951–52 series in Australia … But after [the] 1954–55 series his Test record was … depressed: 13 matches, barely 300 runs, and only 23 wickets. The selectors had to ask the tough question – did they still think Richie Benaud could make the step from Sheffield Shield to Test class?

The selection process that immediately followed the Ashes series defined what sets real cricket selectors apart from armchair cricket selectors. Instead of committing Rich to Test cricket oblivion, [selectors] Bradman, Ryder and Dudley Seddon maintained faith.

They chose him for the 1955 tour to the West Indies. You can ask me, as a one-time Australian selector, whether I would have picked him. Of course! Wouldn't you have?

Rich made 246 runs in five Tests and hit a century in 78 minutes at Sabina Park. And he took 18 wickets, but no five-wicket hauls. However, he did get the 'Three Ws' eight times (Weekes – whom the 'keeper had dropped off him in Rich's SCG debut Test – four times, Walcott three, and Worrell hit his wicket).

Do selectors have a hunch, or a gut feeling? How do they think? The good selector has a knowledge born of years of watching and playing against cricketers of every type and every grade.

Bradman, a champion, had an eye for a champion, just as the gifted horse trainer has an eye for a champion thoroughbred. Of course, neither is always on the money. Cricket is an uncertain as the racing game.

If one Test match can really turn a cricketer's career

then it's possible that the Lord's Test of 1956 did the trick for Rich.

One of the cricket writers covering that tour was Arthur Mailey, the former Test player and wily leg-spinner. This is from his Second Test report in *The Daily Telegraph*:

'Richie Benaud's 97 at Lord's yesterday was a great challenge to modern cricket. Here at least was one player who was prepared to sacrifice a century – his first at Lord's – for the sake of his side.

'Benaud was the last line of the aggressive school of Australian batsmen … thanks to a series of beautiful shots, he reached 97, at which point he tried to hit a six and lost his wicket.

'People around me said: "Wasn't it a pity he didn't reach his century?" Bob Wyatt, an ex-England selector, said to me: "What a terrible stroke - his feet weren't in position".

'I staggered from the scene like a drunken man. Here was a batsman who had climbed to the nineties during a very dangerous period for Australia. He had played every shot from an agricultural swing, to hitting a Fred Trueman bouncer over square leg with a glorious hook shot, to a French cut.

'And at the first mistake he was being condemned.'

KEN BARRINGTON BATTING WITH
RICHIE BENAUD AT SLIP, AND WICKET
KEEPER BARRY JARMAN, DURING A
SURREY V AUSTRALIA MATCH PLAYED
AS PART OF THE AUSTRALIANS' 1956
ENGLISH TOUR. (CENTRAL PRESS/GETTY
IMAGES)

SECOND TOUR OF ENGLAND FOR BENAUD

Cumberland all-rounder Richie Benaud has been selected for his second tour of England with the Australian XI. He was in Hassett's team on the last tour, and followed this up with a successful tour of the West Indies. Benaud, in the West Indies, knocked up the fastest Test century ever scored by an Australian. In the Mailey-Taylor Testimonial, at the Sydney Cricket Ground this season, he gave his critics something to chew over when he slaughtered some of the country's best bowlers in a typical hurricane century. He topped off a great season by captaining NSW to victory over Victoria in the final Sheffield Shield match and winning the shield for his state. The team will leave Perth by sea for England in April.

— THE CUMBERLAND ARGUS, 15 FEBRUARY 1956

PRAISE BE TO BENNO!

You say it, Benno … You shout it, Benho … You spell it, Benaud.

Let us now praise the famous innings that Richie Benaud, the rangy Australian who looks like a blond Viking, played here today.

Before he strode to the wicket he asked Ian Johnson, 'What do I do, skip?' Johnson replied, 'Just as you like. Fling your bat if you want.'

And what a magnificent fling!

— THE ARGUS, 5 MAY 1956

BENAUD HAS NOTTS ON RUN

Richie Benaud, in the brilliant form he showed in the West Indies, had Nottinghamshire on the run at lunch today. In the pre-lunch play Nottinghamshire lost four wickets for 60 and were seven for 237. The wicket, which was dead for the first two days, was now taking spin, and Australia was right on top. Benaud and Davidson completely bewildered the Nottingham batsmen with their well-flighted spinners. Although the match is certain to be drawn, the honours go to the Australians, who never gave up trying on an unresponsive pitch.

— THE ARGUS, 16 MAY 1956

THE TOURING AUSTRALIA CRICKET TEAM IN ENGLAND IN SEPTEMBER 1956 (LEFT TO RIGHT): RON ARCHER, JACK RUTHERFORD, IAN JOHNSON, KEITH MILLER, KEN MACKAY, ALAN DAVIDSON, LEN MADDOCKS, NEIL HARVEY, IAN CRAIG, RICHIE BENAUD AND JIM BURKE. (POPPERFOTO/GETTY IMAGES)

Richie Benaud raises his bat as he comes in to lunch after 90 runs not out in June 1956. (PA/AAP Images)

ALAN DAVIDSON

from an interview with Daniel Lane

I played against him in club cricket, played alongside him for NSW in 1949 and then Australia. I liked that he always had a positive attitude because I was the same – we liked to take the initiative.

We'd been to England in '53, the West Indies in '55 and in '56 we got vapourised [in England] but after we got home Richie and I talked. He worked as a journalist in *The Sun* newspaper office and I'd catch the train to Central and we'd catch the tram to Anzac Parade together and walk with our gear to the SCG.

On this particular day he asked 'why is it the English bowlers can put a ball anywhere they like?' The reason, he said, was because Alec Bedser bowled 1100 overs a year in his County season – that wasn't counting Test matches.

We decided during that 1956–57 summer, which was a domestic season, that we'd bowl unchanged from 4pm until 6.30 … unchanged … and, believe me, by the time you got to 6pm you saw stars and all sorts of things! I had to remind myself 'back foot, front arm' and I'd talk to myself so I knew where the ball would pitch. Richie, well, he reached the stage where he could bowl blindfolded.

We went to Africa in '57–58 and both of us scored over 800 runs. He took 100 wickets, I took 72 and all of the work we'd done over that previous eight months made us what we were. Richie's view was the only way you could get accuracy was by bowling, bowling, bowling and working on technique.

It is a curious and little-known fact that Richie Benaud owed virtually all the success of his career … to his good fortune in contracting dengue fever in India in the winter of 1956.

Two months later he found himself in a place called Timaru in New Zealand, where Australia were playing three unofficial Tests. Benaud, then relatively unknown, owed his selection partly to the sudden demise of Jack Iverson, a mysterious spin bowler plagued by demons (he later committed suicide).

Noticing a local chemist, he walked in and asked a gentleman called Ivan James for sulphanilamide, to stop him blacking out. James noticed bloody lacerations on Benaud's fingers; Benaud explained he was a spin bowler, and these cuts were ruining his career. At which point James, who had treated many ex-servicemen for ulcers caused by gassing, suggested he tried something called Oily Calamine lotion. This Benaud duly did, perfecting the art of healing and protecting the spinning fingers that would bring him to greatness.

I have always thought it wonderful to think that, had he reached over with his left hand in that Timaru chemist … you and I would most likely never have heard of him.

— AMOL RAJAN, THE INDEPENDENT, 10 APRIL 2015

Like most leg-spinners he had to serve a long apprenticeship and that took him into his late twenties before he became a real force in international cricket but the long years of 'grooving' his bowling were not wasted.

At Lord's, in 1956, I had Richie caught behind first ball, and he was given not out. He went on to score 97 (batting at No.8) which proved absolutely decisive and, to a major degree, was responsible for Australia winning the Test.

— FROM *ARLOTT AND TRUEMAN ON CRICKET*

RICHARD COOKE

from *Cricket's Permanent Witness*

Richie made his New South Wales debut on the final day of 1948. Three years later, against the West Indies at Sydney, he first played for Australia. His selection was frequently questioned in those early years, when much other flowering talent was evident in domestic cricket.

In 1952–53 Benaud played against South Africa, recording a duck and having his front teeth smashed while fielding at gully in the Sydney Test, which coincided with his honeymoon. It was not the first time he had been hospitalised by a blow to the head. Four years previously he had been hit in the face while batting for New South Wales 2nd XI in Melbourne.

Then came the 1953 tour, the first of three he was to make to England as a player. In his three Tests he averaged just three runs with the bat – scoring 15 runs over five innings – and took two wickets for 174 before ending the long tour in glory with 135 in a festival match at a crowded Scarborough ground, hitting 11 sixes to equal the world record at that time.

Against Len Hutton's dominant England tourists in 1954–55 he again did little with bat or ball, just as he struggled in 1956 on his second tour of England, the Lord's Test apart: having taken a memorably sharp reflex catch in the gully to dismiss Colin Cowdrey, Benaud was at his cavalier best in an innings of 97, ended by a top edge as he tried to reach his hundred in the grand manner by hooking Fred Trueman.

On the way home Benaud finally fulfilled his potential by taking 7 for 72 (this remained his best Test return) at Madras to set up an Australian innings victory over India, the short series being sealed at Calcutta in the third Test when Benaud took 11 wickets for 105. Having helped Australia win the 1955 series in the West Indies (Benaud's century in Jamaica, one of five in an innings of 758 for 8 – still Australia's highest total in Tests – came in a mere 78 minutes), after four years and 27 Test matches it was felt at last that he truly belonged in the side.

His performances in South Africa in 1957–58 reinforced that belief. Often bare-headed, and a somewhat stooping, rangy figure at the crease, he cracked a century in both the Johannesburg Tests, averaged 54 in the series, and took 30 wickets at a rate of just under 22 runs each in the five Tests. Time and again he and fellow bowler Alan Davidson took the opposition by storm, and the Australians, led by 22-year-old Ian Craig, finished the tour unbeaten.

RICHIE BENAUD SHOWS HIS BOWLING STYLE IN 1956.
(PA/PA Wire/AAP Images)

IT'S WORTH THE WAIT, RICHIE!

Richie Benaud is now a Test hero but he's taken a long time to make the grade. In 17 innings against England he has now made 282 including his 97 today. Benaud defending doesn't look good, but attacking with discretion he's dynamic – AND WAS HE DYNAMITE IN THERE YESTERDAY!
Mackay and Benaud did everything asked of them.

— The Argus, 26 June 1956

BANG… BASH… BANG WENT RICHIE BENAUD

Richie Benaud put the second Test 'in the bag' for Australia today. He knocked up 97 runs to give us a commanding lead on the fourth day of the match, at Lords. We were all out for 257 in our second innings, giving us a lead of 371. England had nine hours to bat, at the rate of more than 40 runs an hour if they were to win. England has never scored 300 in the fourth innings of a Test match. At tea, they were 0–26.

Benaud this morning erased his long line of Test batting failures against England. He exploded the Trueman myth, hitting him for six. Nobody had hooked Trueman for six at Lord's before, let alone in a Test match at such a crucial moment.

Benaud then turned his guns on Statham, Bailey, Wardle, and Laker, scoring runs at better than one a minute. Bailey got the worst beating, three consecutive balls going for four. At the other end, 'Mr Immobility' Mackay viewed the scene in smiling delight.

— The Argus, 26 June 1956

CONNECTION WITH BENAUD

Penrith can justly claim some of the honour and glory being showered upon the Australian cricketer, Richie Benaud, who did so well in the recent test match. His grandfather and father were former residents, the latter being an outstanding cricketer too. Grandfather Richard Benaud was the first secretary of the Agricultural Society, whilst Lou Benaud, father, was a school teacher, who could justly claim a world record as a bowler when in two innings against a St Marys team he took 20 wickets. There's no doubt about where Richie secured his skill.

— Nepean Times Penrith, 28 June 1956

AUSTRALIAN ALL-ROUNDER, RICHIE BENAUD,
BOWLING DURING A MATCH IN SYDNEY.
(HULTON ARCHIVE/GETTY IMAGES)

A.G. MOYES

from *Benaud*

Good length, admirable control and Benaud became inseparable companions. He brought his bowling under the control of his mind. He could not only see the weaknesses in the batsmen but could also lay them bare, and he had the equipment to experiment until he got results ... a variety which gave the batsmen no peace of mind.

He could change his method of attack without faltering in length and direction. He introduced more and more tricks as he developed his art. It was fascinating to watch him grow to bowling maturity.

Benaud has never believed in giving the batsman any rest. He is attacking all the time, and using much variety in that attack. His top-spinner and his bosie are surprises, not props. He is never so mechanical that the batsman will know what to expect. He has been helped also by his ability to make the ball bounce a little higher. Perhaps his height has been an advantage here, but many batsmen have told me that they were confused and defeated more by the ball's bound than by its flight, length and break. Maybe it has been a combination of all these virtues which has so often confounded them.

Benaud has always been a thinker. No slow bowler can reach the top of the hill – it is a difficult upward climb – without much planning, perseverance and hard work. There is no proper pathway to success except through blood, sweat and tears, for the spinner must learn to take a hiding without giving ground. Purposefulness, endurance and brains are prime necessities. Benaud has these qualities, and that is why he finally emerged from the clouds into the sunshine of rich and continuous success. He is without doubt one of the most gifted slow bowlers in cricket's long history.

Richie was one of those sort of people who was always willing to assist you, give you advice but at the same time he was a great mate and I was fortunate as I came into cricket not long after Richie came in. It was in South Africa and he was absolutely fantastic to me.

My big recollection of him, probably my first, was watching him practice. I was only 16 practising in the NSW team and I would go and practise at the ground and there would be Richie and Alan Davidson bowling for two hours and when they weren't bowling they were batting, and from that I took the guidance that they gave me and it helped enormously.

I think what impressed me more than anything was just how easy he did it all. He didn't try to go in for all the fancy stuff, stuck really to the lines of what's the best for cricket and what's best for this team that I'm playing for. So on that regard he was an ideal man to have as a hero.

— BOB SIMPSON, INTERVIEWED BY DANIEL LANE, ESPNCRICINFO

[I recall as the 16 year-old captain of a South African touring schoolboy cricket team] ... being comprehensively 'done' by Richie Benaud. ... I'd never seen a leg-spinner. There weren't many around where I grew up. We were at Lord's playing against a strong Taverners side. I played Benaud reasonably comfortably for a while. Then he bowled me one a fraction shorter. I lay back to cut it and before I knew it, the ball had hurried through and castled me. Benaud called it his flipper.

— BARRY RICHARDS, FROM *SUNDIAL IN THE SHADE*

CAPTAIN

Richie Benaud was the most successful of the post-war Australian captains and no Englishman would complain about that. He was an extremely shrewd and thoughtful leader and his belligerence was expressed in the way he handled his forces, not through the agency of his powers of invective! He was always an aggressive captain because he believed in attacking, but his methods were not simply oppressive.

— FROM ARLOTT AND TRUEMAN ON CRICKET

AUSTRALIAN CAPTAIN,
RICHIE BENAUD IN 1961.
(AAP IMAGES)

A.G. MOYES

from *Benaud*

When Richie Benaud became captain of Australia in 1958–9 he took over a shaky concern. Australia had been beaten in England in 1953; thrashed in Australia in 1954–5; ground into the dust, particularly at Leeds and Old Trafford, in England in 1956. Our cricket was at a very low ebb. In fact, the tide was right out.

Of the eleven who played for Australia against England in the first Test of that [1958–9] series, Benaud, McDonald, Burke, Harvey, Mackay, Davidson, Grout, Meckiff, Burge and Kline had been regulars in the Tests in South Africa. To them was added the gifted O'Neill, who had been so transcendent in the previous Australian season. Benaud had been a very distinguished member of this team, but there is a difference between membership and leadership, especially when one is a star bowler and all-rounder. Then again, Benaud had had little experience in captaincy, and we must not forget that a Test against England is the toughest thing in cricket. This series was against an England which had won three in succession and which was brimful of confidence, scornful of any suggestion that it could be beaten.

Benaud and the Australians, invigorated and inspired by their successes in South Africa, had other ideas. Benaud as leader came through with infinite credit, and his team supported him handsomely. At Brisbane in the first Test there was a good deal of shadow-sparring, as when two boxers test out one another's strengths and weaknesses; but there was also evidence of planning, of a tactical scheme in which every member of the team knew what was required of him. During the match pressure was applied and maintained. The Australians won comfortably. The legend of invincibility was smashed. From that time on there was never any doubt about Benaud's capacity to lead. Even as a comparative novice he had demonstrated clear superiority over an adversary who had had wide and varied experience. It was obvious that the future of

Australian cricket was safe in his hands.

If Benaud did not start the big revival he certainly helped materially in laying the foundation for it, and he built a magnificent structure on that foundation. There is no need to make extravagant claims on his behalf. We all know and applaud his inspiring work. It needs no embellishing. The facts speak for themselves. From the time he took over in 1958 he nurtured among his teammates the conviction that they could achieve the seemingly impossible, both in state and international fixtures. He showed them that he had abundant faith in them. And they had the same faith in him. That's why matches were won when defeat seemed at least possible and sometimes probable.

Mostly in life and in cricket a man makes his own luck. It stems from the capacity to know and understand men and matters; of having a will to succeed; of being prepared to go a little further along the road that leads to the point of no return. Benaud has been fortunate at times – some victories achieved against the law of probability suggest this – but mostly he has come through because he had a proper appreciation of his team's potential and of the frailty of the opposition. That was his blueprint for success.

Benaud is the finest captain I have seen since Bradman. There are … many points of similarity between them. Neither has lost a series. Both have tried to win instead of merely seeking not to lose. Both could estimate probabilities and plan ahead. Both could alter their tactics to meet changing circumstances. Both were positive.

AUSTRALIA'S CRICKET CAPTAIN, RICHIE BENAUD, TALKING
WITH SIR DONALD BRADMAN DURING THE FAMOUS TIED
TEST AT THE GABBA BETWEEN AUSTRALIA AND THE WEST
INDIES. (THE COURIER-MAIL/NEWSPIX)

Benaud told Bradman he was going to chase a win, 'I'm pleased to hear it,' Bradman said.

A.A. THOMSON

from *Cricket: The great captains*

If Bradman had been a hammer to crush the English, Benaud was a mosquito to sting them. In his three victorious rubbers against England he did not so much crush them as tease them into defeat. ... when May in 1958–9 took out what seemed a particularly strong side it was Benaud who rallied what had been Australia's scattered tanks and turned the tide of the battle in their favour.

In each series, too, there were some outstanding performances by the captain himself, either in bowling or the art of strategy, which turned the scale. No other Australian captain [until then] has won three successive rubbers against England. (Bradman, of course, won three, but the sequence included the drawn rubber of 1938.)

From the very first he began to make his mark against May's men. In the first Test his bowling had much to do with England's undoing and though it was Meckiff who did the damage in the second game, it was Benaud, with nine wickets in the third match, who forced England into a position where they were fairly fortunate to draw. The fourth Test, at Adelaide, saw Benaud's men batting first, sent in by May in a last attempt to salvage the series, but the effort was in vain. As in all three previous games, Australia's batting, though vulnerable, could always find both someone to dig in and someone to score quickly, while England still could not find an opening pair and had to rely far too much on May and Cowdrey. Again Benaud took nine wickets in the match, and was in fact more deadly than the faster bowlers whose jerky action had looked, to say the least of it, doubtful. In the fifth Test Benaud won the toss for the first time in the series and, seemingly for the sake of variety put England in to bat. Once more, with melancholy monotony, the batting faltered and failed. The faster Australian bowlers broke through to start with and then it was Benaud who finished the first innings off. England, whose ranks had been depleted by a car accident to Statham and Loader, tried desperately hard and, despite a stubborn hundred by MacDonald, were coining near to even terms when the sixth Australian wicket fell at 209. But then as has so often happened, even as late as at Headingley in 1964, the attack, bowling and fielding alike, seemed to lose all grip and direction and a fierce onslaught by Benaud and Grout put on 115 for the seventh wicket. Thus England's final effort was crushed. There still remained stout rearguard actions by Cowdrey and Graveney and some spectacular hitting by Trueman but all to no avail.

So Benaud won his first rubber of captaincy against England in almost as convincing a manner as Armstrong's in 1920–1. He had batted courageously when runs were most wanted, though he needed only one innings per Test, and bowled more consistently than anyone on either side for his 31 wickets. (Laker had been England's most reliable bowler with less than half that number.) What was most remarkable was that the touring side, who looked good on paper and had initially been backed to win, were in the outcome not good enough, whereas Australia, who were not necessarily superior, man for man, seemed to have already been welded into a smoothly functioning team under a captain whose example persuaded everybody on his side to field better than they had ever fielded before.

Australian captain, Richie Benaud, shaking hands with England captain, Peter May, following the Australian victory in the fourth Test match at Adelaide in February 1959. (Keystone/Getty Images)

Australia's Alan Davidson is caught by West Indies wicketkeeper Gerry Alexander off the bowling of Gary Sobers (right); batsman Richie Benaud looks on.
(AAP Images)

MALCOLM KNOX

from *The Captains*

[In 1960] the game was facing growing criticism about slow batting, slow over rates and chucking. Its popularity had received a transfusion from television, but this also attracted even more attention to the excesses of defensive play.

Now secure as captain, Richie Benaud resolved to do something about the game itself. With Frank Worrell, captain of the West Indians touring in 1960–61, he made an informal agreement to play entertaining cricket and to hell with the results. The series, and Benaud's part in promoting it, has been documented to exhaustion. It helped that the West Indians bristled with personality: Worrell, Wes Hall, Rohan Kanhai, Garry Sobers, Conrad Hunte, Joe Solomon, Cammie Smith, Lance Gibbs. It also helped that the First Test in Brisbane had the most exciting finish in cricket history.

Benaud's contribution to the tie was telling. Directing traffic, he moved catchers in at the first sniff of weakness, and left them close when the West Indian batsmen tried to spread them. At tea break on the last day, when most watchers thought Australia, six wickets down, would settle for a draw, Benaud told Bradman that he was going to chase a win. 'I'm very pleased to hear it,' Bradman said.

Benaud personally led the Australian chase, adding 134 with Davidson and only getting out, hooking, in the last over. Three balls later Solomon threw down the stumps for the second time from side-on and the match was tied.

The best of his career hung principally on the exhilarating Test series of 1960–61, when he captained Australia against the visiting West Indies side led by Frank Worrell. Some tedious contests had been inflicted on the watching public, with more to follow in the 1960s. But that extraordinary five-match encounter produced electrifying batsmanship, and bowling that was less concerned with shutting the game down than keeping it moving.

The opener at Brisbane delivered the thrill of cricket's first tied Test match. At Adelaide, a nation was brought to a standstill during a long, pulsating last-wicket stand between Ken Mackay and the near hopeless No.11 Lindsay Kline as they secured an unlikely draw for Australia. When, a few months later in England, Benaud took veteran Ray Lindwall's advice and bowled his leg-spin around the wicket into the rough, when all seemed lost in the Old Trafford Test, his wicket-taking that afternoon ensured that Australia retained the Ashes and raised the captain close to sainthood in the estimation of his team and his country.

— DAVID FRITH, THE GUARDIAN, 10 APRIL 2015

In Brisbane, character and temperament clothed the dry old bones of cricket with flesh and blood for the first time for years. By modern standards, either side, at some stage in the past two days' play, should have played for a draw. Neither did. The result, true poetic justice, was that neither won.

The winner, as Richie Benaud has said, was cricket itself.

— SYDNEY MORNING HERALD, EDITORIAL, 18 DECEMBER 1960

CRICKET'S NEW LOOK THANKS TO… RICHIE BENAUD, SPORTS STAR OF 1960

Test captain Richie Benaud is the *Sun-Herald* choice as sportsman of 1960. This choice of a team player is made in a year of notable achievements by individual performance. Benaud's claims are not that in 1960 he had surpassing success as a spin bowler.

The remainder of the Australian summer, followed by the summer in England, might even show that he is past his high noon as a bowler – although spinners come to full maturity late. Benaud now is 30.

His outstanding achievement in 1960 was to gain mounting recognition of his belief that cricket after all is a sport and should be played as such. While seeking to win, Benaud does not regard the game of cricket as a battle of attrition. He has brought to Australian cricket that badly needed sense of adventure his immediate predecessors as Test captains did not have in their make-up.

The Benaud way probably does offend the cricket purist – why declare so early or at all, for example, instead of making certain of a draw.

Cricket has long and desperately needed the fresh life the Benaud outlook has brought. If from now on the 349 runs on the first day of the second Test and the 375 in the Shield match at the SCG should become the rule rather than the exception no small measure of the cricket public's thanks must go to Richie Benaud.

— SUN-HERALD, 1 JANUARY 1961

The 1960–61 series is unique in that Benaud and Worrell genuinely committed their teams to playing cricket how they would love to play it. They were rewarded with the tie in Brisbane, the most exciting draw in history in Adelaide, when Kline and Mackay held out for 110 minutes, and a series that was squared 1–1 until the last moments of the last match, in Melbourne, when Mackay and Johnny Martin got Australia home by two wickets. Not since 1902 had a more exciting series been contested. Johnny Moyes wrote that the West Indians' effect 'was amazing: they turned the world upside down; they arrived almost unhonoured and unsung; they took away with them the esteem, affection and admiration of all sections of the community. They proved what so many of us had declared – that people will go to see cricket played as a game and an entertainment.' Some 90,800 spectators turned up for the Saturday of the last Test, while half a million people flooded the streets of Melbourne to give both teams an emotional farewell.

I'd first played against Richie when Australia were in the West Indies in 1955 but it was in the 1960–61 series in Australia that I got to really appreciate what a wonderful cricketer and captain he was. [I had] never seen cricket played like it was. The relationship between the teams was magnificent, on and off the field, and we were loved by the Australian people wherever we went. … Benaud, along with Donald Bradman, [then chairman of the Australian board], and West Indies captain, Frank Worrell, created it. From then on, Richie became a good friend. We would get in a round of golf whenever we met. He was someone you got to like as he was always the same, always easily approachable and helpful.

— GARRY SOBERS, INTERVIEWED BY TONY CROZIER, ESPNCRICINFO

Benaud's Calypso Summer crowned his career, notwithstanding being booed in Melbourne for appealing when Solomon's cap fell on his stumps. Benaud took eight wickets in Sydney, and in Adelaide complemented seven wickets with 77 and 17. He was the complete cricketer: captain, batsman, bowler, fieldsman, an international figure whose smiling intelligence transcended his sport.

MIKE COWARD

from *Calypso Summer*

At the close of the 1950s not even Sir Donald Bradman, the most influential cricket person of the 20th century, could mask his fears for the future welfare of Test cricket. Despite Australia's emphatic 4–0 success and the emergence of Richie Benaud as an exceptional leader, the 1958–59 Ashes series was often a turgid affair, and it did little to ease the disquiet of the Australian cricket community.

Cricket was being endured, not celebrated, and spectators hankered for the joyous game played in England by Australia in 1948 and by the West Indies in 1950. It had become a game of attrition, with England, especially, more intent on ensuring that they did not lose rather than determinedly trying to win. Furthermore, it was blighted by wickedly slow over-rates and vexed controversies surrounding 'throwing' and 'dragging'.

There was an urgent need for change; and the game was fortunate in having, at this time, the calibre of men who could effect major change and carry the new standard to the world.

Renowned for his clarity of thought and practicalness, Sir Donald was convinced that a series of exceptional enterprise and entertainment would reinvigorate Test cricket and re-engage the people. To this end he enlisted the services of Benaud, whom he knew to be a friend and admirer of Frank Worrell. Worrell, to the undisguised relief of the international cricket community, had finally been appointed captain of the West Indies team.

Worrell's appointment represented change on a massive scale. He was the first black man to lead the West Indies outside the Caribbean since they entered the Test match arena at Lord's in June 1928.

Suffice it to say that Benaud was happy to conscript Worrell to the cause, and together they oversaw a series that set a bench-mark, and is still spoken about with undiminished enthusiasm 40 years later.

Such was the significance of the series and its impact on the entire cricket world that Sir Donald sought the approval of his board to create the Frank Worrell Trophy for future competition between the teams.

RICHIE BENAUD AND FRANK WORRELL FROM THE WEST INDIES TOSS THE COIN TO BEGIN PLAY. (AAP IMAGES)

ALAN DAVIDSON

from an interview with Daniel Lane

He was a great assessor of the game. With Richie it was never a risk but always a calculated decision to do something. Nobody ever analysed or knew the opposition like Richie did and it was the same thing with his own team – he knew what every player in the side could do and that allowed for him to make decisions which, to the outsider, who wasn't a cricket expert, seemed 'different'.

Richie could assess a situation quickly, it wasn't so much waiting for a coach to send a message out because he acted mid-over. I bowled long spells for him on many an occasion ... he was a brilliant captain, a joy to play for – you have no idea.

He always had the ethics of cricket in his mind. There was never a scene with any of the players when he was captain. Never any ill-feeling, no bad behaviour.

Whenever a bloke lost his cool and started to carry on Richie said 'that'll be enough' and it stopped immediately. It was the happiest time I know in cricket because he moulded together a group of blokes who became a good team. We had Norman O'Neill, Bob Simpson, Neil Harvey, Peter Burge and Bill Lawry. It says a lot that a player as good as Brian Booth struggled to get into the team.

We had a great team and when you have a brilliant tactician and a man who was always confident, it's not hard to realise why success followed.

It was a wonderful time of cricket. We went to Africa in '57–'58; we played England in '59, toured India and Pakistan in 1959–60 and hosted the West Indies here in 1960–61. Test cricket was rejuvenated in that series by two men who were wonderful people, Frank Worrell was an amazing person, as was Richie ... it might sound unheard of now but we went out socially with our opposition in the middle of a Test match.

The legacy of the leadership by both captains is the camaraderie ... if we meet the West Indians today we don't shake hands, we bear hug. The mateships continue 55 years later.

JOHN BUCHANAN

from *Learning from Legends*

You could describe Richie as the first modern cricketer. Flamboyant and charismatic, with shirt unbuttoned virtually to the waist, he and his teams played attacking cricket, changing the image of a game that some thought had become boring.

He and the West Indies captain Frank Worrell and their teams breathed new life into the game with the thrilling 'Tied Test' series of 1960–61.

Richie's decision to keep going for the runs on the final afternoon of the Tied Test in Brisbane – even when the Australians were six wickets down with 140 runs still to get – made that match the history-making event it was. And he led from the front, scoring 52 to take his team to the brink of victory.

The following year in England, he turned around another seemingly lost cause, this time with the ball.

With England cruising to victory at Manchester, Richie made the virtually unprecedented move of bowling his leg-spinners around the wicket. It was a gamble, but if he did nothing the game would have been almost certainly lost. It worked. He immediately dismissed the rampant Ted Dexter and two balls later bowled English skipper Peter May behind his legs for a duck.

Richie finished with six wickets, England lost its last nine wickets for 51 runs and Australia won the match and retained the Ashes.

'I've never known anyone who was a completely natural leader; you have to work very hard at it because you are totally responsible for what happens to your team.

'If people talk of someone being a completely natural captain, they are having a lend of themselves and of the person concerned. I found the most important thing in being captain was to stay two overs ahead of the play. If you are level with what's going on, or an over behind, then the opposition will run all over you.

'It was Keith Miller who taught me to stay ahead of the play, and it was great advice.

'Leadership revolves around being in charge of a group of people, welcoming their ideas and suggestions and, at the same time, having them completely understand you will be the one making the final decision.

'The reason you will have the final say is that, while you might be the one taking some credit, you will certainly be the one taking all the blame if anything goes wrong. If your decision/gamble/guess doesn't work out, don't be shy about saying to them, individually or as a group, that you might have been better off thinking again about their suggestion.'

ON LEADERSHIP

Good leaders read the game and always stay ahead of it.

Welcome ideas and suggestions but make the final
decision yourself.

Listen and watch! Listen and remember!

Do your best.

Never give up.

Don't take yourself too seriously.

Always be honest with your players because they are relying on you making
decisions that will keep them in the team.

Remember, you are only one of the team.

— RICHIE BENAUD FROM *LEARNING FROM LEGENDS*

MALCOLM KNOX

from *The Captains*

Yet he was wearing out. His right shoulder had been so overworked on the subcontinent and at home that by 1961 he could only brush his teeth and shave with his left hand. When he became captain, he took up smoking. He seldom seemed affected by the pressure, but he would have been inhuman not to feel it.

On the 1961 tour Benaud would take 61 wickets, second to Davidson, and score 627 runs at 25.08. But his peak years had come between two Ashes tours; England never saw his best. To compensate for his decline, teamwork was again his credo: for the first time, eight bowlers captured more than 50 wickets on a tour.

Under Benaud at Headingley, Harvey produced some of his best batting, top-scoring in both innings with 73 and 53, to stand alone in the ultimately vain battle to stave off defeat.

The teams went to Manchester tied 1–1. A tight match swung England's way in the fourth innings when, chasing 256, they reached 1–150, Dexter flaying Davidson and Mackay. Benaud took a punt and brought himself on to bowl around the wicket. Shane Warne would later make a specialty of bowling into the rough created by the fast bowlers' footmarks, but in 1961 it was a novelty. Looping leg-spinners were asking to be smacked behind square, but Benaud had nothing to lose. Better a lucky captain, he would later say, than a good one. Or, as Derbyshire fast bowler Harold Rhodes said, 'If you put your head in a bucket of slops, Benordy, you'd come up with a mouthful of diamonds.' Benaud, like Taylor after him, believed in the mystique of his own luck and thereby caused others to believe as well. At Edgbaston, two balls after moving Lawry into an unorthodox short gully for Mike Smith, Lawry had the catch and the legend of Benaud's magic grew another chapter.

Benaud got one to pop on Dexter, bowled May around his legs second ball, and spread such panic in the England changing room that the match was over in a session. England's last nine wickets dissolved for 51 and Benaud finished with 32–11–70–6. It was his greatest afternoon as a Test match bowler.

His other achievement at Old Trafford was to pair Lawry with Simpson. Even after his breakthrough 1960–61 Test season, Simpson gave himself reason to believe he was no favoured son. An automatic pick for the 1961 tour, he had been shifted down the order. His renewal as a cricketer had come as an opener, but he was falling victim to his own versatility. His returns at six were moderate until, in the second innings at Old Trafford, he opened with Lawry facing a deficit of 177. They put on 113, launching Australia's matchwinning lead. Like had found like. Over the next six years, Simpson and Lawry would establish an opening bond that was recognised as the best Australia had known.

Lawry's popularity as a reliable and, yes, exciting new Australian opener with a penchant for crunching hook shots would never exceed its 1961 levels. He was known as a practical joker, nailing Benaud's boots to the floor and also swiping one of the Queen Mother's teaspoons, depositing it in the pocket of the put-upon tour manager, Syd Webb. Such stories would astonish those who later knew Lawry as a colourless, dogmatic warhorse.

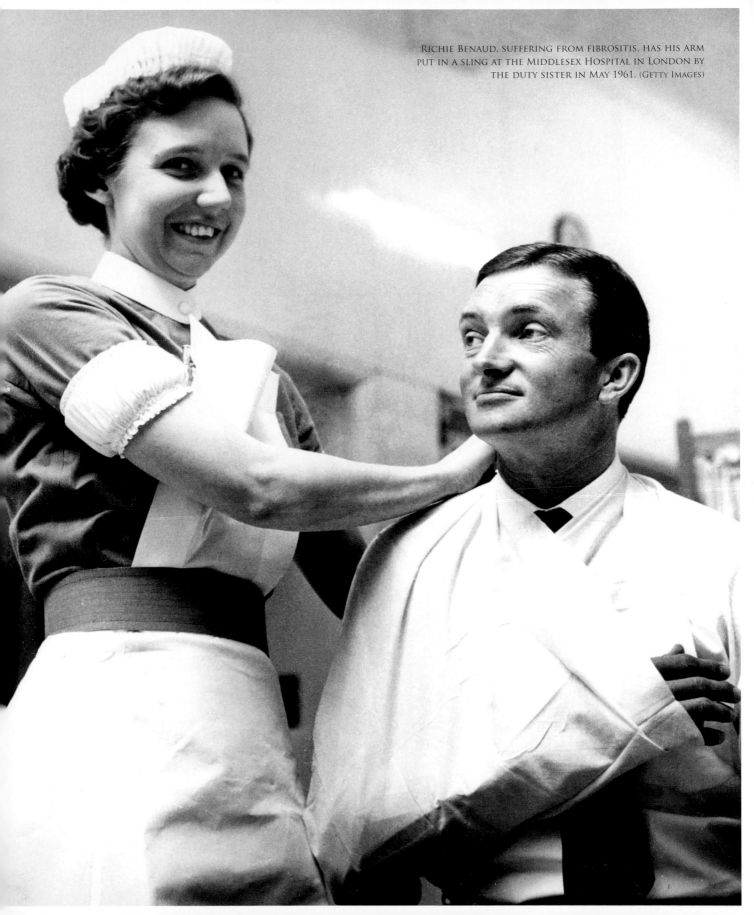

RICHIE BENAUD, SUFFERING FROM FIBROSITIS, HAS HIS ARM PUT IN A SLING AT THE MIDDLESEX HOSPITAL IN LONDON BY THE DUTY SISTER IN MAY 1961. (GETTY IMAGES)

VICTORIOUS ASHES TEAM CAPTAIN RICHIE BENAUD SHAKES
HANDS WITH THE CHAIRMAN OF THE AUSTRALIAN BOARD
OF CRICKET CONTROL, SIR DONALD BRADMAN, WITH TEAM
MANAGER MR. S.G. WEBB, ON ARRIVAL BY SHIP TO ADELAIDE
IN OCTOBER 1961. (VERN THOMPSON/NEWSPIX)

[But] Benaud led the tour under a cloud of petty Board politics. Benaud was too friendly with journalists, inviting them into the changing room, for Webb's liking. The Board applied a gag to Benaud, who protested directly to Bradman. Their combined influence was enough to soften the Board. As if to drive home their sympathies, *Wisden* named him a cricketer of the year and the Queen gave him an OBE.

WISDEN CRICKETER OF THE YEAR

1962

If one player, more than any other, has deserved well of cricket for lifting the game out of the doldrums, that man is Richard Benaud. Captain of Australia in four successive and triumphant series to the end of 1961, he has demonstrated to enthusiasts all over the world that the intention to make cricket, particularly Test

cricket, attractive and absorbing is every bit as important as skilled technique in batting, bowling and fielding. He has succeeded in his aim to re-create interest in cricket because he loves playing it.

The New South Wales State selectors, ever on the look-out for rising talent, first picked him when 18 as a batsman and this was still his primary role when promotion to international status came his way at the age of 21 in the fifth Test Match against West Indies at Sydney in January 1951.

Thus far, his ambition had been realised, but he had no means of knowing that almost 10 years later, against the same country, he would lead Australia in the First Test match tie in history. Meantime, Richie Benaud came to England in 1953 and 1956 and he also earned representative honours against South Africa, India and Pakistan. His gradually mounting bowling skill was evident on his first two English trips, but he is remembered chiefly during those ventures for the dashing 97 he hit off the England attack in the second Test at Lord's in 1956.

The 1957–58 tour to South Africa at length established him as an all-rounder of top class, for he took 106 wickets,

which surpassed the previous record of 104 by S.F. Barnes, and scored 817 runs including four centuries, two of them in Test matches.

Ian Craig led Australia in this series, but the following year slow recovery from illness precluded his choice for the captaincy against England when they toured Down Under. So Benaud, somewhat to his surprise, but very keen to put his many theories into practice, was appointed to the task of recovering the Ashes which England had held since Hutton wrested them from Hassett in 1953.

Benaud duly completed his mission and fully justified the selectors' faith in him despite fears that the burden of captaincy might affect his form. His fine bowling, which yielded him 31 wickets for 18.83 runs apiece, proved a major factor in Australia's triumph of winning four Tests and drawing the other. Shrewd and inspiring captaincy transformed an ordinary side into an invincible combination bent on revenge – and gaining it.

Eight Test appearances in India and Pakistan a year later and five more during the memorable visit of West Indies to Australia in 1960–61 – all as captain – brought Benaud's total of caps to fifty. In India and Pakistan he excelled by taking 47 wickets (average 20.19) in the Tests

The West-Indian team celebrates as Australia's Ian Meckiff is run out with only two balls to go, during the first Test at Brisbane in December 1960. The match ended in the first ever tie. (Photo by Central Press/Hulton Archive/Getty Images).

BENAUD'S SCHEME PRAISED

England must take up the Australian challenge for brighter cricket or give up Tests. This is the opinion of Mr R.W.V. Robins, one-time captain of England and Test selector and one of the game's boldest campaigners, as quoted by the *Daily Mail*'s cricket writer.

In a series of questions and answers, Robins described Richie Benaud's attractive cricket challenge as 'magnificent'. He said Benaud was the first Test captain to say he would persist with his plan of attractive cricket no matter how his opponents played. Obviously, the object of the game was to win – but not by any means, Mr Robins said. Mr. Robins said the 'real issue' this summer turned on the willingness of a side to risk defeat to achieve victory, instead of the recent policy of thinking victory only when safe from defeat.

— THE CANBERRA TIMES, 26 APRIL 1961

RICHIE BENAUD AND DUKE EXCHANGE TIES

The Duke of Edinburgh and Australian cricket captain Richie Benaud exchanged ties at the Lord's Taverners spring luncheon, in the Long Room at Lord's yesterday. The Duke presented Benaud with a Lord's Taverners tie with which goes honorary membership of the Taverners.

Handing his tie to the Duke, Benaud said: 'I have here an Australian tie which was not in existence in '56 when the last team was here. This tie has been through Test series against South Africa, India, Pakistan, England and West Indies, and it has not lost a series. If I may say, Sir, I would like you to have it, I have another with which to start another era of victory.' (Laughter.)

Benaud, referring to the Duke's prowess as an off-spin bowler, aroused laughter when he said: 'Our rather illustrious selectors have left this side without an off-spinner ... I was hoping that you perhaps might be persuaded this afternoon to twirl one or two overs at us.'

The Duke said: 'I think the Australian Test series is really something special for all of us, and for everyone who loves cricket and for a great many others who like the hard-fought campaign.'

— THE CANBERRA TIMES, 28 APRIL 1961

and in the ensuing exciting rubber against Worrell's West Indies team he was second in the wicket taking list with 23 to the evergreen Davidson's 33.

Having with Worrell flung down the gauntlet to those who considered Test matches could only be grim affairs, Benaud consolidated his position as a cavalier captain when he visited England for the third time as a player last summer and helped his men to retain the Ashes.

His inspirational value was graphically demonstrated by the fact that although he missed nearly one-third of the matches – including the second Test – through shoulder trouble and was handicapped in some others, the Australians won the series 2–1 and maintained an unbeaten record outside the Tests.

When Benaud arrived in England with his team he pledged them to play attractive cricket – winning or losing. He also promised more overs to the hour as an antidote to defensively minded batsmen or bowlers. He promised quicker field-changing and fewer time-wasting tactical conferences during play.

He and his men did their best to carry out his positive policy, and their faster scoring alone proved a telling reason for the success of the tour. When unable to lead his team, Benaud planned strategy with Neil Harvey, his able and wise vice-captain.

Pain, for which he had injections, did not deaden Benaud's intense desire to conquer on an English visit. That his playing share was limited to 32 innings for 627 runs and 61 wickets for 23.54 apiece spoke eloquently of his influence and worth in other directions. Nevertheless, his contribution of six wickets for 70 in the second innings of the fourth Test at Manchester when the issue of the match and series lay in the balance, was a traditional captain's effort made at a crucial time. He explained the achievements of his side by declaring that they had risen to the occasion, but, modestly, sought no credit for his part in them.

It was a great pity that, because of his shoulder injury, Benaud could not give his admirers last summer other than rare glimpses of his best form, but he had already done enough to make sure of a high place in cricket history. He came with the reputation of being one of the finest close-fielders in the world – either at gully or

RICHIE BENAUD HITS A NO-BALL FROM FREDDIE TRUEMAN FOR TWO DURING THE FIRST TEST AGAINST ENGLAND AT BRISBANE ON 7 DECEMBER 1962. (ALLSPORT HULTON/ARCHIVE/ GETTY)

MAGNIFICENT TEST GAME – CAPTAINS' SUMMING UP

Rival captains Richie Benaud, of Australia, and Peter May, of England, last night summed up the fourth Test at Old Trafford as a 'magnificent match'. But Britain's newspapers, while applauding Australia's great fighting win to retain the Ashes today, blasted England for its lost opportunity and poor batting. 'Benaud Benefit Day … England's Heart Torn Out in 20 Minutes of Deadly Skill' were the headlines blazed across the sports page of the *Daily Mail*.

Only 14,000 people saw Australia snatch a dramatic, spine-tingling 54-runs win yesterday but the five days play attracted an Old Trafford record aggregate of 133,000 of whom 72,458 paid at the gate.

'It was the best game I have played in since I took over the captaincy,' Benaud said last night. 'We were a bit busy out in the middle, but it must have been very gripping for the spectators.'

The dejected May, stunned at the way the Australians turned a certain defeat into a great victory, paid tribute to Benaud's efforts in the field, including his 6–70. 'Richie's performance was a great one and I am the first to congratulate him … Altogether it was a great game of cricket,' May said. The England skipper said his players had been instructed to get the runs but could not cope with Benaud. The Australian captain said his only worry yesterday was that the team might relax when it had England on the run. But they did not. 'They were like tigers in the field,' he said. Benaud offered no comment on individual Australian efforts because 'we play as a team and not as individuals.' But he said that Ted Dexter's 76 for England was one of the finest innings he had seen in Test cricket.

— THE CANBERRA TIMES, 3 AUGUST 1961

BENAUD SETS TEST RECORD

Australian captain Richie Benaud set a Test record when he dismissed England captain Peter May in the fifth Test today. He brought his total of dismissals in Test cricket to 263, one more than the 262 dismissals of England's Alec Bedser. The only other player to have topped 250 is Australia's Ray Lindwall, with 254. The dismissals are made both bowling and in the field.

— THE CANBERRA TIMES, 18 AUGUST 1961

in a silly position – and appreciative of the hazards thus entailed he would never ask a man to take up a dangerous post he would not himself occupy.

As a forcing batsman, Benaud, tall and lithe, has always been worth watching. His drives, powerfully hit and beautifully followed through, are strokes of especial joy to those whose day is made if they see a ball sent hurtling over the sightscreen. At Scarborough in 1953 Benaud hit eleven 6s and nine 4s while making 135.

Still it is as a bowler that Benaud, in recent years, has touched the heights. An advocate of practice and yet more practice, the erstwhile youngster from the backwoods has long had a bulging quiver of arrows for attack.

The urge to trick the batsman has developed in Benaud the ability to evolve many more ways of getting a man out than his four basic deliveries. Changes of pace and flight, with the ball released from different heights, angles and lengths, have combined to make Benaud a perplexing rival for the best of batsmen. He really likes bowling as it affords him more chance than batting to keep in the thick of a fight he relishes.

A fighter, indeed, he has been all through his cricket career which nearly came to a tragic end almost before it had begun when, as a youngster playing for New South Wales Second XI, he suffered a fractured skull in failing to connect with a hook stroke. Fortunately, he recovered to bring pleasure to cricket followers all over the world and to attain a place among the great players, a distinction earned by his taking of 219 wickets and scoring 1744 runs in 54 Test matches to the end of 1961. Only three other Australians – M.A. Noble, Keith Miller and Ray Lindwall – have scored 1500 runs and taken 100 wickets in Tests, and Lindwall alone (228) has captured more wickets for Australia.

AUSTRALIAN CRICKET CAPTAIN,
RICHIE BENAUD, AND
ENGLAND SKIPPER, PETER MAY,
IN 1961. (NEWS LTD/NEWSPIX)

As a young man he advised me: 'Ian, it's a simple game. The simpler you keep it the better off you'll be.'

— Ian Chappell

RICHIE BENAUD, SENDS DOWN A BALL, DESPITE THE
REPORTED FIBROSITIS IN HIS SHOULDER, IN MAY 1961.
(AP Photo/AAP Images)

IAN CHAPPELL

from *Fifty-two Years with Benords*

'After you, Ian.' They were the first words spoken to me by Richie Benaud.

It was 1962 and South Australia had just enjoyed a rare victory over a star-studded New South Wales line-up. Benaud, as the not out batsman, magnanimously stood back to allow Les Favell's team to walk off the Adelaide Oval first. I was on the field as 12th man and wasn't about to leave ahead of the Australian captain and a man whose leadership style I'd admired from afar, but he insisted.

That story is indicative of Benaud. He was a thorough gentleman and meticulous in his preparation – I was staggered he knew my name.

He was also a generous man. Not long after the Adelaide Oval experience, a Gray Nicolls bat arrived in the post while I was playing in the Lancashire League. It was from Richie, and so began a relationship [of] 52 rewarding years.

I say rewarding; that was from my perspective, but I'm not sure what Benords received in return. Often when I spoke to him or called, he had a helpful suggestion, which emanated from a mind that was regularly in lateral-thinking mode.

As a young man he advised me: 'Ian, it's a simple game. The simpler you keep it the better off you'll be.'

When I became captain I called to explain how a mate had said: 'You've got the field in the wrong place for [Garry] Sobers.'

He laughed. 'There's no right place for the field when Sobers is going,' he explained. 'All I'd say is you're wasting a fieldsman putting someone in the gully. He hits the ball in the air in that direction, but it's six inches off the ground and going like a bullet. No one can catch it.'

LAST TOUR OF ENGLAND

Australian Test captain, Richie Benaud, said today that he would not be available for any future touring teams after this visit to England. Though this means he is now leading his last touring team Benaud said his decision did not mean the end of his international career. He said that he would like to go on playing in Australia for the next few seasons but future tours as a player were definitely out.

Benaud now is leading his second touring team since being appointed captain in 1958. He has lost only two Tests in the three series since 1958. One was lost to India and the other against the West Indies in the recent series.

— THE CANBERRA TIMES, 24 MARCH 1961

RICHIE BENAUD PREPARING TO BAT.
(W. PEDERSEN, NATIONAL ARCHIVES OF AUSTRALIA)

RIC FINLAY

from *My Richie Era*

I know where I was on November 30, 1962, because my database tells me. I was at home in bed afflicted with the cursed bronchitis that frequently interfered with my primary education. I know this because it was the first day of the 1962–63 Ashes series at the Gabba, and Richie was captain of Australia. I must have had some idea of cricket before this date, but I have no memory of it. That day, therefore, marked the start of my conscious cricket life.

I was permitted to have my mother's transistor radio, and I tracked the performance of the Australian batting that day in my father's ABC cricket book – but not accurately enough for him. He noted that I hadn't entered the batsmen in the order in which they batted, and I was made to rub it all out and start again. My first scoring lesson.

Brian Booth made 100 that day (112 in fact: I can still remember the individual scores made that day without recourse to a scorecard), and thus became my first cricket hero. In this day of high-definition TV and slow-mo, I find it amazing that a child can generate heroes in his mind without the images that would seem to be essential. Radio still has its place in developing a strong affinity with the game, even with the very youngest. It may not be a coincidence that radio has been the dominant environment in what I call my cricket career.

Booth was out before the day's end, and Richie came in. Not out overnight.

I remember my disappointment when Richie retired the following season. I had only caught the tail-end of his career, of course, but that was my first brush with the phenomenon of retirement, and the first realisation that cricketers don't play for ever. I sulked for a week.

ENGLAND CAPTAIN TED DEXTER IS ABOUT TO OPEN A BOTTLE OF CHAMPAGNE TO TOAST AUSTRALIA'S EIGHT-WICKET WIN IN THE THIRD TEST MATCH AT SYDNEY. (AAP IMAGES)

RICHIE BENAUD LIFTS NSW TO GREAT WIN

NSW and Australian captain Richie Benaud, in one of the greatest bowling spells of his career, today captured seven MCC wickets for 18 runs at Sydney Cricket Ground. His effort enabled NSW to beat the MCC by an innings and 80 runs. This was the first time NSW had beaten an English touring team by an innings.

Benaud was criticised for closing the NSW first innings at lunch at six for 53 giving them a first innings lead of 184. Many critics thought he should have batted until tea for a big first innings lead because NSW had last use of the wicket. Benaud quickly silenced his critics when he dismissed the MCC for 104, about an hour before stumps. Benaud finished the day with seven for 18 off 18 overs, including 10 maidens. Only nine scoring strokes came from his bowling.

The NSW total of 512 was the highest the State had scored against an MCC team for 38 years. The MCC spinners received no turn from the wicket this morning but Benaud and Martin made the ball turn and lift sharply in the afternoon.

— The Canberra Times, 20 November 1962

Owing to a bus strike only about 6,000 spectators watched Richie Benaud's last day on a Test cricket field, the final day of the series between Australia and South Africa at Sydney Cricket Ground in February, 1964.

But the 6,000 did their best to make up for absent friends in giving Ritchie a fitting farewell. They clapped him at every conceivable opportunity. They applauded him the whole way to the wicket as he walked out to score three runs, three more than Sir Donald Bradman scored in his final Test innings. They applauded him all the way back to the historic pavilion. They applauded him when his successor Bobby Simpson thoughtfully allowed him to lead Australia on to the field for the fourth innings of the match. They applauded him when he came on to bowl his first and his last overs. They thronged around him to cheer him off the field.

And he left that field outwardly as unemotional as ever but, as he later confessed feeling a strong and painful tug at his heart – that giant heart which had served Australia so superbly and gallantly in many a Test crisis.

— R.S.WHITINGTON FROM *BRADMAN, BENAUD AND GODDARD'S CINDERELLAS*

JOURNALIST

Prominent Jamaican cricket officials last night defended the fiery West Indian bowler, Charlie Griffith, against strong charges, hacked by pictorial evidence, that he is a 'chucker'. The pictures … were taken by former Australian captain Richie Benaud, who is covering the series for Australian newspapers.

The photographs graphically depict Griffith with his arm bent behind his left ear in a 'slinging' pose. His left foot is turned out towards point, and his body is front on. The photographs show Griffiths' bent arm suddenly straightened at the point of delivery … The pictorial evidence could bring to a climax the controversy that has surrounded the 26-year-old Barbadian giant in recent years.

— THE CANBERRA TIMES, 9 MARCH 1965

BENAUD

Richie Benaud, the former Australian Test captain, is to be chairman of the Cricket Writers' Club next year when the Australian team may stay in England after the proposed World Cup to play a series of Test matches. It is the first time that the club has had a chairman from another country.

— THE CANBERRA TIMES, 16 JULY 1974

GIDEON HAIGH

The beginnings of Benaud's career ... date back to an era when the proprietor was always deserving of his honorific. He experienced his first media urges in the early 1950s when he was a junior accountant in the 'counting house' of the Fairfax media group in Sydney.

He would drift upstairs to the offices of *Sporting Life* magazine where Keith Miller held court with three first-class cricketers turned journalists, Dick Whitington, Ginty Lush and Johnny Moyes. Benaud would think: 'This is the most exciting thing. I'd love to be able to write like all these guys.'

Benaud applied annually for a reporter's job ... For six consecutive years the editor Lindsay Clinch turned him down, not weakening until Benaud arrived home from a successful 1956 Ashes tour.

Benaud recalls their interview with such evident enjoyment that he even permits himself a profanity.

'I s'pose you've come in to ask about your application to join editorial,' said Clinch.

'Yes, Mr Clinch.'

'When did you get back?'

'Last night.'

'That's pretty keen.'

'I'm pretty keen to do it, Mr Clinch.'

'Why is that?'

'I want to learn to be a journalist.'

'You want to fucking learn to be a journalist. Everyone would like to learn to be a journalist, particularly some of those who are writing on this paper!'

For the first few years of his career Benaud was apprenticed to the paper's star police roundsman Noel Bailey, chasing fires, car crashes and even the odd murder. Listening to Bailey dictate copy of perfect length from payphones with minutes to edition taught him the importance of not wasting a word: something that still characterises his plain, spare prose as well as his concise commentary.

Working as a columnist while Australian captain made him the object of some suspicion from a hidebound and parsimonious Australian Board of Control. In an age when Test cricketers seem to be issued a column with their cap it seems astonishing that Benaud was in his time barred by board statute from writing about any match in which he was involved, even when he dashed off 15 excited paragraphs for *Sydney's Sun* after the tied Test in 1960–61.

'I got a letter from Barnesy [the board secretary Alan Barnes] in the next post,' Benaud recalls. It said: "I wish to remind you that you have broken by-law so-and-so by writing about what occurred in a day's play. Please do not do this again or the board will have to take action".'

When freed by retirement from the board's dictate, Benaud made tough calls as a journalist. He was at the forefront of criticism of Charlie Griffith's bowling action 40 years ago; he backed his brother John in a celebrated dispute with the New South Wales Cricket Association over footwear in 1970; he boldly fronted Kerry Packer's breakaway World Series Cricket in 1977. As years have passed, however, his pronouncements on the game have been less trenchant, more Delphic.

Richie was a lot of fun. But there's a better way of putting it. I was a cricket fan from way back and I first saw him play when I went to Headingley on the '53 tour. I was still at school in England, I thought the English team were boring, but the Australian team had so much spark. I thought 'gosh'. By '67 we were married and it was a partnership right from the very beginning. We were writing all the time, doing the journalistic thing and television.

— DAPHNE BENAUD, SUNDAY TELEGRAPH

FORMER AUSTRALIAN CRICKET CAPTAIN RICHIE BENAUD WITH FORMER MISS DAPHNE SURFLEET AFTER THEIR WEDDING AT CAXTON HALL, WESTMINSTER, LONDON. (AAP IMAGES)

MAX PRESNELL

from *In the newsroom*

Humanity more than charisma stood out for Richie Benaud in Sydney's murky world of police rounds reporting late in the 1950s.

The circulation war between the afternoon dailies *The Sun* and *Daily Mirror* made Ben Hecht and Charles MacArthur's *The Front Page*, regarding Chicago newshounds, look like a comic strip. Opposition car tyres were punctured and public telephone wires torn out of sockets by reporters in their lust for a scoop, or even a time edge regarding an edition.

In October 1959, the big story was the recapture of Leslie Allan Newcombe, who had been on the run from Long Bay for 13 days with galloping mate Kevin Simmonds. The search was described as 'Australia's biggest manhunt', a title possibly given enhancement by a hack. However, Newcombe was to be put on display at the Criminal Investigation Branch headquarters, accompanied by Ray Kelly – Sydney's precursor to Clint Eastwood's Dirty Harry – to make sure further flight was impossible.

Every copper at the CIB gravitated to *The Sun*'s Richie Benaud – unsurprisingly, because he was Australia's cricket captain and they were enthusiastic to give him any special insight or colour he required.

Meanwhile Frank Crook, then a first-year cadet with the *Daily Mirror* and on his first major assignment, was left in the dust of the stampede. When the pictures were taken and the police figured Richie had had his fill, Newcombe and the law departed just as quickly.

Benaud walked over to the young reporter and said: 'Get your notebook out'. Crook was given every quote and angle Richie had secured exclusively. 'We wouldn't have done it,' Crook, who made his mark in journalism and broadcasting as well as a stint as a cricket writer, related when the situation was discussed recently. He was spot on.

> When I was made captain of New South Wales, and then Australia in 1958, I decided to do it my way. I was a working journalist with *The Sun* newspaper in Sydney on police rounds under Noel Bailey, and was writing a sports column. At that time the Australian Board of Control – aptly named – and the players were miles apart: master and servant was the relationship. No media man was permitted to enter the Australian dressing room. I changed all that. From the first Test at the Gabba in Brisbane on 5 December 1958, the press were welcome to come in and talk to the players in the dressing room to gather background information, but they weren't allowed to quote the players. They could quote me, but not my team. Otherwise, the innovation would instantly cease.
>
> My appointment had been by no means unanimous, and I heard later that this madness of fraternising with the press confirmed the worst fears some of the board members held when I was named. In fact, Australian cricket had never had better publicity. We won the series and then came the 'Tied Test' series against West Indies and the 1961 tour of England, all very successful.
>
> — RICHIE BENAUD, FROM *LEARNING FROM LEGENDS*

FORMER AUSTRALIAN CRICKET CAPTAIN, RICHIE BENAUD, ON THE WAY THROUGH BRISBANE IN MARCH 1964, TO COVER THE TEST TOUR OF ENGLAND. (GEOFF MCLACHLAN/NEWSPIX)

Former Australian Test cricketers, Ian Chappell,
Bill Lawry, Bob Simpson and Richie Benaud in
Melbourne on 20 September, 1977 promoting World
Series Cricket. (Fairfax)

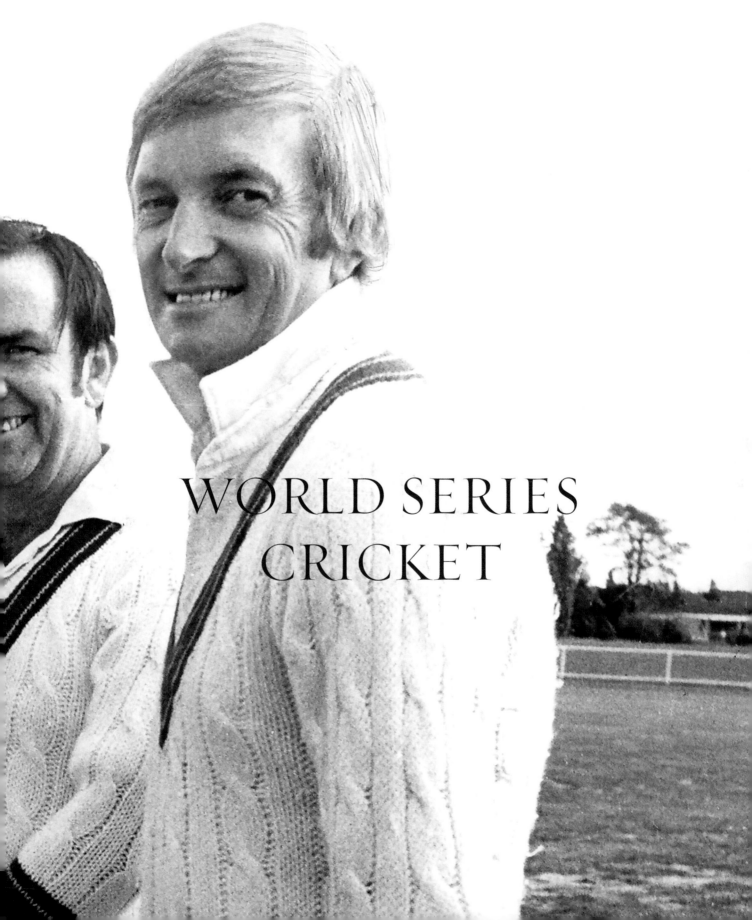

WORLD SERIES
CRICKET

DENNIS LILLEE

on World Series Cricket

The seeds of the idea that became World Series Cricket were sown during a meeting I had with John Cornell in a Perth hotel. The subject of payment to players – or the lack of it – was discussed. My original idea to improve our lot was to have the best Australian players play a one-off game against the best of the rest of the world.

John took the idea to Channel Nine mogul Kerry Packer, who initially saw it as the opportunity to televise some cricket. But the idea of a one-off game grew into a series of games pitted against the Australian Cricket Board, as it was known then, and this eventuated in Packer getting big-time cricket on his network.

At the time it was all very exciting – and very hush-hush. Behind the scenes I was regularly consulted about the players to be approached and was occasionally asked to convince some of the overseas players that Kerry Packer was a man of substance who really meant business. I was committed. Totally. But there were times in the developmental stages that I couldn't help standing back and wondering if we were all doing the right thing.

Until, that is, I was told that Richie Benaud was on board. I knew then that we as players had made the correct decision. Such was his standing in the cricketing world. If it was good enough for Richie to be involved, it certainly was good enough for everyone. If he thought that what we were doing was right for the future of cricket and for cricketers, then our decision was validated. Plus, I knew then that we'd be in good hands, because of his incredible cricket brain.

I didn't see much of Richie in the very early days, but I kept hearing of the impact he was having at management level. He was very much hands-on there, and I believe that almost everything he suggested was taken on board. It was no surprise to me that we as players didn't see a lot of him then. Richie wasn't the sort of guy who wanted to be in the front seat when the photographs are taken. As time got closer to the first game, though, we would see him at various group functions.

As we started to put the product on the park, he and I would have the occasional one-on-one. He was very interested in knowing how we were handling the new concept, which was a really compact season. We were constantly playing and on the road. Making it even more difficult for the players, usually there were no real practice facilities – and, because of bans by traditional cricket, we weren't able to go back to state or club teams for match practice if we were out of form. It was a totally new scenario and Richie wanted to know how we were coping. I guess so that he could take information back to senior management.

For me, and the rest of the players, Richie was a steadying influence in often-turbulent times.

DENNIS LILLEE PREPARES TO BOWL. (PATRICK EAGER)

RICHIE BENAUD. FORMER AUSTRALIAN CRICKET CAPTAIN
AND COMMENTATOR. (Fairfax)

DANIEL BRETTIG

from Benaud, the effort behind the effortless, ESPNcricinfo

Benaud was 26, and a four-year fringe dweller in the Australian Test side, when the 1956 Ashes tour concluded, England having kept the urn for a third consecutive series. Most of Ian Johnson's unhappy teammates could not wait to get home, but Benaud stayed on after asking the BBC if he could take part in a course of television production and presenting. By that stage, he was already working as a police roundsman for *The Sun* in Sydney, chasing ambulances when he was not honing his slowly developing leg-breaks.

The broadcasting and journalism apprenticeship Benaud put himself through was exhaustive and exacting. He grew gradually in grasping the finer points of each trade, and would combine both when he stepped away from playing eight years later, having matured brilliantly as a cricketer and a captain. Cricket and leg-spin had taught Benaud about the level of commitment and perseverance required to succeed – as Bill Lawry has recalled, other players admired how Benaud emerged, not as a natural but a self-made man.

When Kerry Packer's World Series Cricket emerged from its clandestine origins in 1977, Benaud's broadcasting apprenticeship paid off in much the same way as his cricketing one had done. More than 20 years of experience in broadcasting with the BBC and the ABC, among others, meant that he was not only Nine's host and lead commentator but also a sort of consulting producer, someone able to give direction to a crew ostensibly at the ground to direct him.

The polish of Nine's broadcast was there largely because Benaud had applied it himself, with the help of a gifted pair of brains behind the camera in David Hill and Brian Morelli. Having lived through the hectic earlier overnight shifts at *The Sun* and austere days learning the ropes at the BBC, broadcasting the cricket on Nine was a challenge well within Benaud's range – his unscripted introductions and summaries were as assured and comprehensive as those of the very best broadcasters.

If anything, he was too careful about expressing his opinions, a trait his more outspoken brother and fellow journalist John was never shy in offering a good-natured ribbing about. Nevertheless, Benaud's care with words reflected that he had learned much by spending time writing and speaking on the game. He knew the power of word and image, and made doubly sure he would be prepared enough to make the most of both.

Such dedication is commonplace among professional cricketers, and has become ever more so with each generation following on from the World Series Cricket revolution. But the path Benaud followed from playing into broadcasting has become the road less travelled, if at all. While so many within and without the game will say how much they loved and admired Benaud's work, precious few can be said to have made a genuine fist of following his example.

[Ian] Chappell is one such figure, having worked assiduously at his writing down the years though never being trained formally as a journalist. Another, Mark Nicholas, travelled the world as a cricket correspondent for various publications including the *Telegraph* while still playing for Hampshire, and has clearly tried to take after Benaud as much as possible.

DAVID HILL

from Most searching cricket coverage ever

How TV will cover the World Series Cricket ...

We're going to turn our cameras on them and tell you why. We are going to make cricket come alive. From the dressing room to the wicket in the centre of the ground, we will keep audiences constantly in touch with what's going on. Instead of feeling that they are sitting in a remote seat in the outer, TV viewers will be right alongside the umpires or walking beside a dismissed player on the way back to the dressing room to face critical mates. We think the game is drama, pathos, humour, excitement and a lot of hitherto unanswered questions the fans want to get to the bottom of.

We've spent about a million dollars on new equipment – we are even inventing some. It's too technical to mean much to the viewer in words, but the results will be startling. We can go from a distant, wide shot of the ground, right into show a spot on the nose of the guy at the wicket.

We're experimenting with mics buried in the ground next to the wicket, just to pick up the death rattle that every batsman knows when the stumps are skittled. I want viewers to hear the sound before they see the picture and shout: 'He's out!' Or the sound of a snick going through. There's always the hours-long argument did he snick it with his bat or did it hit his pad? We'll have radio mics on the umpires so the viewers can hear them say 'yes' or 'no'. You'll be able to see the batsman's face.

We are conscious that it is a game of cricket. We can't slow, speed up or alter anything. It remains a game of cricket played by the top men in the world. I've talked to the cricketers. They haven't kicked about anything, but had more suggestions themselves. They are happy.

Our commentary will be more vigorous than past TV. Richie Benaud and Keith Stackpole will look after that. It will be fantastic in prime time when people can come home and sit down to watch the best cricketers in the world. The big lights in VFL Park, Waverley Melbourne are high and strong enough. I've been a TV sports producer for years now and this is the big one. I can't wait for it to start.

AUSTRALIAN TYCOON. KERRY PACKER SURROUNDED BY MEDIA IN 1977. (JOHN MINIHAN/EVENING STANDARD/GETTY IMAGES)

BENAUD, CHAPPELL TURN ADMINISTRATORS

Richie Benaud and Ian Chappell, two of Australia's most successful cricket captains, will hold administrative positions with Kerry Packer's World Series Cricket in Australia this summer. Benaud is on the five-man governing committee, while Chappell, captain of Australia in the series, will be one of the two players' representatives, it was announced yesterday.

The other players' representative will be chosen when all the overseas players assemble in Australia for the series. Two other former Australian Test players, Bob Cowper and John Gleeson will join Benaud on the government committee with chairman Brian Treasure, the administrative controller of World Series Cricket, and Geoff Forsaith, a former grade cricketer in both Western Australia and NSW. A spokesman for World Series Cricket said: 'The three former Test players on the committee bring a wealth of practical cricket experience to the series. They have been selected for their knowledge of the game and the need to maintain traditional standards.'

He also announced the signing of two more Australian players, Western Australian opening batsman Bruce Laird and former Australian and South Australian off-spinner Ashley Mallett. Mallett retired from first-class cricket last season after missing selection in the Australian team for the first Test against Pakistan. Laird showed great early season form and looked a likely tourist to England, but his form slumped and he failed to gain selection.

The first match in the World Series, between Australia and the West Indies will be played at VFL Park, Melbourne, from November 24 to 27.

— The Canberra Times, 20 September 1977

AUSTIN ROBERTSON

from *Richie Benaud, Daphne, Kerry Packer and Me*

World Series Cricket would have certainly failed without the genius of curator John Maley, Kerry Packer's money and television network, Dennis Lillee's vision, John Cornell's savvy – but just as important as all of those were Richie and Daphers.

Rich was WSC's Rock of Gibraltar. During WSC's crises, and there were plenty, Rich always had his hand on the tiller. The Benaud fingerprints were all over every subtle move, and nothing ever fazed him. His guidance and input were paramount.

Rich had a saying that he often used: 'Stay icy calm'. Many people under extreme pressure will grunt, yell, curse, die a thousand deaths and live a lifetime in a moment. But, in moments of extreme pressure, Rich would stay as cool as a cucumber. That sort of calm is a powerful force. Rich was the WSC's sedative, and there's no way we would have succeeded without his cool wisdom, along with Daphers, his strong right arm.

If he was ever disappointed in something you did he would give you that whimsical look and, in a slightly higher-decibelled voice, say: 'Ocker, stay icy calm'. I was probably more familiar with that unsettling look than anybody. Rich was a gentle man, with a telling, uncompromising, 'she'll be right, folks' attitude to everything.

Prior to the start of WSC, Rich assisted me many times. After signing the players, securing John Maley

as the curator (that was my own most important contribution), grounds, doctors, players, kit and anything else you can think of, the mind of Kerry [Packer] turned to the commentators.

Kerry and Rich decided that Bill Lawry had to be a part of the team.

'Fix that Austin,' Kerry ordered. Well, sure, easy peasy, but was I in for a shock … Rich gave me Bill's number, and I called him.

'Hi Bill, my name's Austin Robertson, we have met before …' was as far as I got.

'Austin Robertson? What are you ringing me for?' and he slammed the phone in my ear. Undeterred, I rang him straight back.

'Now Bill, hang on a second, it's Austin again, and I am ringing on behalf of Richie Benaud.'

'Well, that's different,' said Bill, and we know the history from there.

This was just a tiny example of the Benauds' bond, pure and simple – a wonderful, lifetime commitment from one person to another.

We knew it would take time. Packer was not one to give up easily. This is where he got it so right. He got experienced and knowledgeable people around him, many of whom were former players.

— BARRY RICHARDS, FROM *SUNDIAL IN THE SHADE*

KERRY PACKER WITH TONY GRIEG AT THE DORCHESTER HOTEL IN 1977. (AAP IMAGES)

In the years before the World Series Cricket breakaway, Ian and I, as Australian captains, had addressed the Board about issues that concerned us. It wasn't just a plea for better pay, though that was part of it. When gate receipts alone were exceeding $1 million a Test match, it cost the board $200 a player to put us on the field. The sacrifices we had to make to play cricket drove many of our best players out of the game.

World Series produced so much that was positive: innovations in the game to make it more attractive, better conditions for players, the emergence of several new stars, and some of the best cricket anyone had been involved in. It had given South African stars such as Barry Richards, Mike Procter, Clive Rice, Eddie Barlow and Garth le Roux a chance to show their talents on the big stage.

— GREG CHAPPELL FROM *FIERCE FOCUS*

[Benaud] criticised the poor rewards for the cricketers of his time, claiming they were 'not substantial enough' and that 'some players… made nothing out of tours'. He contended as far back as 1960 that 'cricket is now a business'.

Those views obtained active expression when he aligned with World Series Cricket – it 'ran alongside my ideas about Australian cricketers currently being paid far too little and having virtually no input into the game in Australia'. Benaud's contribution to Kerry Packer's venture, both as consultant and commentator, was inestimable: to the organisation he brought cricket know how, to the product he applied a patina of respectability. Changes were wrought in cricket over two years that would have taken decades under the game's existing institutions, and Benaud was essentially their frontman.

In lending Packer his reputation Benaud ended up serving his own. John Arlott has been garlanded as the voice of cricket; Benaud is indisputably the face of it, in both hemispheres, over generations.

— GIDEON HAIGH. THE WISE OLD KING.
WISDEN ASIA CRICKET MAGAZINE 2002

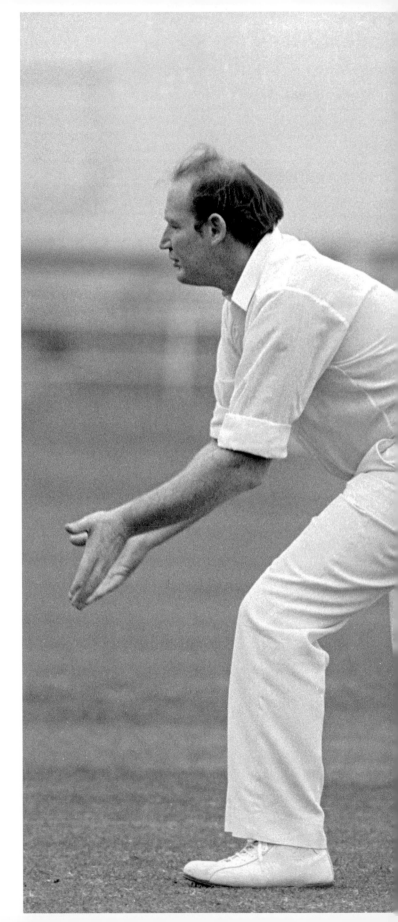

A PRESS CRICKET MATCH. ENGLAND V AUSTRALIA, ON THE REST DAY OF THE HEADINGLEY TEST IN 1977. KERRY PACKER, DAVID FRITH AND IAN CHAPPELL FIELD IN THE SLIPS. (PATRICK EAGAR/PATRICK EAGAR COLLECTION/ GETTY IMAGES)

RITCHIE BENAUD,
CRICKET COMMENTATOR.
(PA Photos/AAP Images)

DENNIS LILLEE

The Melbourne Cricket Ground holds wonderful memories for me. The nature of the venue and the atmosphere created when it was full of screaming fans would give me a huge lift. I took more wickets there (82 from 14 Tests) than at any other venue.

Eleven of those wickets came in the fabled 1977 Centenary Test against England, which Australia managed to win by a narrow margin. While for obvious reasons I'll never forget that game, there were two other special personal memories for me at the 'G'. The first came when I broke the Australian record for the number of wickets taken in Tests and the second, when I broke the world record.

The former was particularly special for me, for a couple of reasons. I had grown up a great admirer of West Australian fast bowler Graham McKenzie. Along with West Indian giant Wes Hall, 'Garth' had been an inspiration to me in the days when I was deciding that I wanted to follow them along the path to pace. And so my antennae were up when I arrived at the MCG for the third and final Test against India in February 1981. At that juncture, just ahead of me in the list of Australian Test wicket-takers was Graham Douglas McKenzie, with 246 next to his name.

I managed to pass my hero's total in the first innings. Cause for minor celebration. Two more wickets and I'd take the Australian record, held by Richard Benaud. When Bruce Yardley took the catch at point off India's Chethan Chauhan, and the record was mine, I turned to the press area and saluted Richie with a thumbs-up signal. I had so much respect for him that I was almost embarrassed to have taken the record from him. But in due course I recognised that through this achievement I had, in a sense, come of age as a cricketer.

Anyway, we were relaxing in the dressing room at the end of play that day when there was a knock on the door – and there was Richie, carrying a bottle of champagne.

There followed a warm smile and handshake and a genuine, 'Well done, Dennis … congratulations'. That meant so much to me.

LILLEE OVERCOMES ALL TO GET TO THE TOP

Last week in Melbourne he entered his 57th Test just five wickets short of the world record held by lanky West Indian spinner Lance Gibbs, and three short of the 307 mark of equally controversial English fast bowler Fred Trueman.

Lillee should have broken the record long ago, but his spell with the breakaway World Series Cricket organisation cost him a probable 29 official Test appearances. In two seasons since the outcasts were reconciled with traditional cricket, Lillee has taken more than 110 wickets.

Lillee, last season, overtook spinner Richie Benaud's Australian Test record amid a controversy not of his own making. On the MCG – his most successful Test venue – in the third and final Test against India, Lillee grabbed his record-equalling 248th wicket when his appeal for lbw against touring skipper Sunil Gavaskar was upheld. Gavaskar trudged slowly off the field, calling Chetan Chauhan off as well, in a protest over umpiring decisions. But the incident ended as Indian manager, Wing Commander Shahid Durrani, ran down the steps and waved to Chauhan.

Minutes later, with the crowd still wondering about the incident, Lillee had Chauhan caught. Lillee signalled to Benaud in the Channel Nine commentary box as his team mates congratulated him. Lillee later explained his signals meant he was now No.1 and Benaud No.2.

— CANBERRA TIMES, 28 DECEMBER 1981

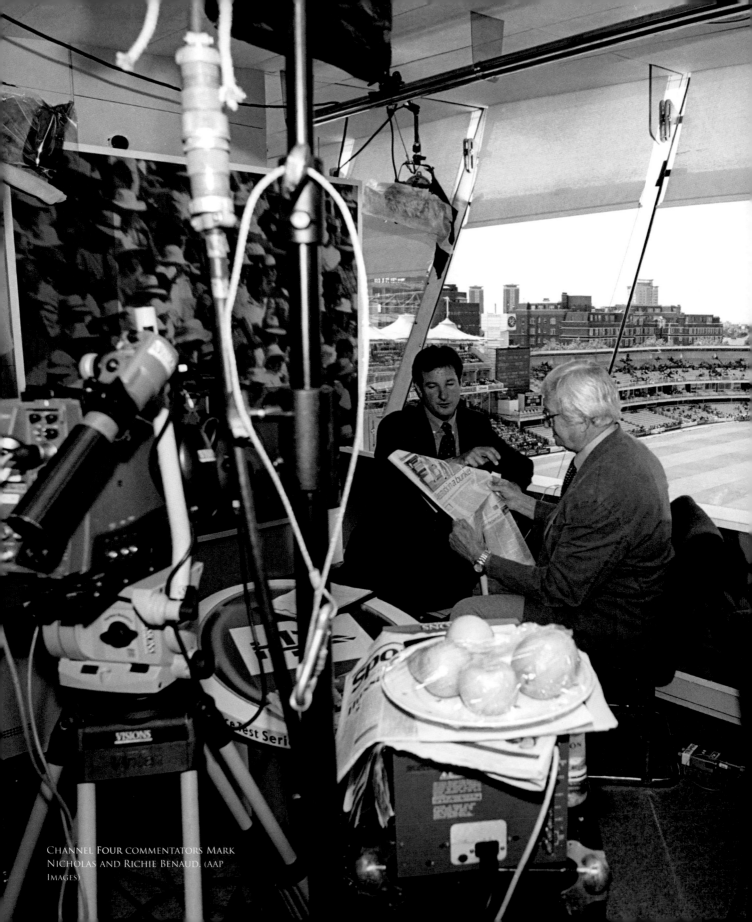

CHANNEL FOUR COMMENTATORS MARK
NICHOLAS AND RICHIE BENAUD. (AAP
IMAGES)

COMMENTATOR

BENAUD'S TIPS FOR ASPIRING COMMENTATORS

Everyone should develop a distinctive style, but a few pieces of advice might be:

Put your brain into gear before opening your mouth.

Never say 'we' if referring to a team.

Discipline is essential; fierce concentration is needed at all times.

Then try to avoid allowing past your lips: 'Of course …' 'As you can see on the screen … 'You know …' or 'I tell you what …', 'That's a tragedy …' or 'a disaster …' (The *Titanic* was a tragedy, the Ethiopian drought a disaster, but neither bears any relation to a dropped catch.)

Above all: when commentating, don't take yourself too seriously, and have fun.

— WISDEN ALMANACK, 2003 EDITION

IAN CHAPPELL

from *Fifty-two Years with Benords*

When I retired and turned my hand to writing and television, he [Richie] organised for me to commentate on the BBC – with whom he'd trained in 1956 – during the 1977 Ashes series. He also suggested (Richie rarely advised) I become a member of the Australian Journalists Association so there would be no objection to me writing columns.

He did offer me advice once. It was the 1976–77 season and we were commentating on the 0/10 [TV] network. Over a drink he told me: 'Ian, there's a better way.' I was eagerly awaiting his thoughts on how I could improve my commentary, when he expanded: 'You don't have to tell every pest to piss off. There is a better way.'

He listed some options but I don't think they registered, as I replied, 'But sometimes I get a lot of satisfaction from telling someone to piss off, Benords.'

The very next day a strange thing happened. I accepted an invitation to lunch with cricket officials, where there was an even stranger occurrence. I told a former schoolmaster of mine who had recently written me a scathing letter that I'd enjoyed reading his missive.

I walked away feeling buoyant and thinking, 'Benords is right; There is a better way.'

When I happily related the incident, he looked at me quizzically and said: 'Then how do you explain what happened to me after play?'

Richie had met a mate in the bar at the cricket ground and no sooner had he enjoyed his first sip of wine than a guy marched over to him and said: 'You don't remember me, do you?'

A pause, another sip of wine, and then Benaud responded: 'Don't tell me. Just give me a few seconds and I'll get the name.'

After a couple of exchanges the guy couldn't contain himself and blurted out his name. 'Well, piss off then,' was Benaud's response.

For a man who lived up to his 'keep the game simple' advice on the cricket field, he had a propensity for complicating golf. I remember when he proudly announced he'd bought an odometer so he could measure courses and distances. I was quick to remind him that his good friend and five times British Open champion Peter Thomson always said: 'It's a hand and eye game.'

However, he did live up to his 'keep it simple' advice as a television commentator and presenter. 'Don't say anything unless you can add to the pictures,' was his mantra as a commentator.

As a presenter, he had that marvellous ability to make it look like everything was progressing without a wrinkle, when in reality all hell was breaking loose in the studio.

In the early days of *Wide World of Sports*, he was opening the telecast at the Gabba when the set fell forward onto the back of his head. Without breaking sentence he slowly pushed back with his shoulders to move the set off his head. At that precise moment his watch alarm started buzzing. Maintaining his composure while issuing a perfect sentence, he surreptitiously reached under his cuff and turned off the alarm.

It was illuminating to hear people's comments on Benaud. Occasionally they would say, 'I love Richie's commentary but it's a pity he hasn't got a sense of humour.' I felt like replying, 'So you watch television but you don't listen to it.'

His was a droll sense of humour and at times it could border on wicked.

RICHIE BENAUD AT WORK ON HIS TYPEWRITER
WHILE IAN CHAPPELL LOOKS ON. (MARK RAY)

DENNIS LILLEE

Of course I knew Richie. Everybody in cricket either knew him or thought they knew him. Such was his stature in the game – and that was not only in Australia! But this day in 1985 was very different. I was about to step out of my world and into his. Don't ask me why, but I had said 'yes' to an approach from Channel Nine to do

a broadcast stint during the India Test at the Melbourne Cricket Ground.

Following my retirement from Test cricket a year or so before, there had never been even an inkling in my mind that perhaps I might make a move into the media. In fact, as a player I'd had a rather jaundiced view of it all. I don't even know now why I accepted, but at the time of the Test I was going to be in Melbourne on other business, so when I was asked I thought 'why not?'

Walking up the stairs to where the broadcast boxes were situated, I couldn't escape the feeling that I'd made a monumental mistake. And when I opened the door and walked into the Nine area, I was sure I *had* made a decision that I'd truly regret. Although I should have felt comfortable enough in just another cricket environment –and, of course, I immediately recognized a number of the faces – my heart was really pounding. My first impression was the actual size of the broadcast box. I couldn't believe that such a small space could produce so many words and so much information. They were crammed in like sardines in a can.

Next thing I knew I was directed to a seat, facing the ground, where the game was under way. Next to the doyen of cricket commentators. The towering personality that was Richie Benaud. Naturally, I'd given some thought as to how this was going to pan out, but, not having watched much cricket on television, I had no real preconceptions about how I should play my part. Add to that dilemma the fact that I'm actually working with the most consummate professional in the business! I'd literally been thrown in at the deep end. Nobody took me to one side and said, 'do it this way'. I was flying by the seat of my pants. Literally. No practice, no training, no journalistic background … I just passed English at school!

There he was, the great man. As I settled into the seat, a beautiful turn of the head and that wonderful warm Richie smile, which I'd got to know well over the years. That helped to settle the nerves a little. Away he went, with the commentary. Then when it was perhaps my turn to say something he just turned and looked at me. So I started talking … and talking … and talking. The next thing he turns back to me and puts a finger to his lips. The clear message: Stop talking! I thought he was only indicating that it was his turn to talk, so the next time it was my turn off I went again … and again, for too long.

I don't know how, but I got through that stint behind the microphone and the next thing I know Richie's sitting next to me at the back of the box. Thank goodness, he was offering me some advice. Golden nuggets. The theme was, 'there are pictures and people can see what's going on … you shouldn't really say too much at all … it's not like radio, where you have to paint the pictures in your own words'. For me, it was a much-needed master class in television broadcasting technique.

Well, the lesson was abruptly interrupted when this guy came up, tapped Richie on the shoulder and said, '30 seconds, mate'. Richie nodded to him and, to my surprise, turned back and continued talking to me. For about 20 seconds. Then he calmly stood up, said 'excuse me' and walked four or so paces to his chair and went on with his spiel – as though he'd been preparing it in minute detail for the last half hour. As far as I could tell, he hadn't seen much of the game at all while he was talking to me, but to my astonishment he not only left it till the last few seconds to take up his position – but then gave the most comprehensive summary of what had happened, as though he'd watched every single ball bowled.

CRICKET COMMENTATOR RICHIE BENAUD HOLDING A
MICROPHONE IN THE BROADCAST BOOTH AT ADELAIDE OVAL
IN JANUARY 1982. (NEWS LTD/NEWSPIX)

JIM WHITE

The Guardian, London 2001

Benaud puts much of his technique – his economy with words, the way he resists the temptation to call the Australians 'we' – down to his training. Not for him the route now favoured by commentators of using their playing careers as a shop window for a move into the media on retirement. He was a journalist by profession. In the days when cricket was no more than a paid hobby.

'I did the midnight rounds for eight years,' he recalls. 'I worked under a fellow called Noel Bailey, he taught me something I could do now – if the phone went and someone said "we need 300 words immediately", I could dictate it. You get this inbuilt thing ticking in your head about the number of words you're doing. Same way as now I've got an inbuilt thing about what time is left and how many words are required to fill it. In your ear you're hearing "25 to go, 20 to go, 10, 9, 8 … " At the same time you can hear people in the gallery shouting at each other … 3, 2 … and you say "good night" on one. And it's just practice, but it's got to work. Doesn't work, you go and do another job.'

'Of course. I remember at Lord's once, a West Indian spectator came on the field and did some acrobatics and I said something about it, and I got a voice in my ear, it was the director. "Lovely story, Richie, one of the best I've ever heard. It would have been awfully nice if I had a camera on it".'

In fact, Benaud says, he still has much to understand about the medium in which he works. 'The best thing I can do after a Test back home is walk up to the shops,' he says. 'Daph, my wife, leaves me to it and goes shopping, while I'm stopped by maybe 50 people who want to have a word. It's a rare day when I don't learn something about the production or my performance. And occasionally it is of tremendous use.'

All the same, there must have been a point at which he realised he was rather a good commentator? 'It's not possible to answer that except by saying I only achieve anything through hard work,' he says. 'But I don't want to say that because it sounds a bit pretentious. In 1956 television started in Aus, but I didn't utilise it until 1963. I watched and studied, kept looking and listening for seven years before I tried my hand at it.'

Ever since, he has lived a dual-hemisphere existence, five months in Australia, five months in England, and the rest of the year in Nice. Nearly 40 years without being cold. '1962 was the last time I saw a winter,' he smiles.

'Did you ever play cricket for Australia, Mr Benaud?' In his *On Reflection*, Richie Benaud recalls being asked this humbling question by a 'fair-haired, angelic little lad of about 12, one of a group of six autograph seekers who accosted him at the SCG.' 'Now what do you do?' Benaud writes, 'Cry or laugh?'. I did neither but merely said yes, I had played up to 1963, which was going to be well before he was born. "Oh," he said. "That's great. I thought you were just a television commentator on cricket." Autograph in hand, the boy scampered away with a "thank you" thrown over his shoulder.'

It is a familiar anecdotal scenario: past player confronted by dwindling renown. But the Benaud version is very Benaudesque. There is the amused self-mockery, the precise observation, the authenticating detail.

In fact, Benaud would rank among Test cricket's elite leg-spinners and captains if he had never uttered or written a word about the game.

— GIDEON HAIGH, THE WISE OLD KIN, WISDEN ASIA CRICKET MAGAZINE 2002

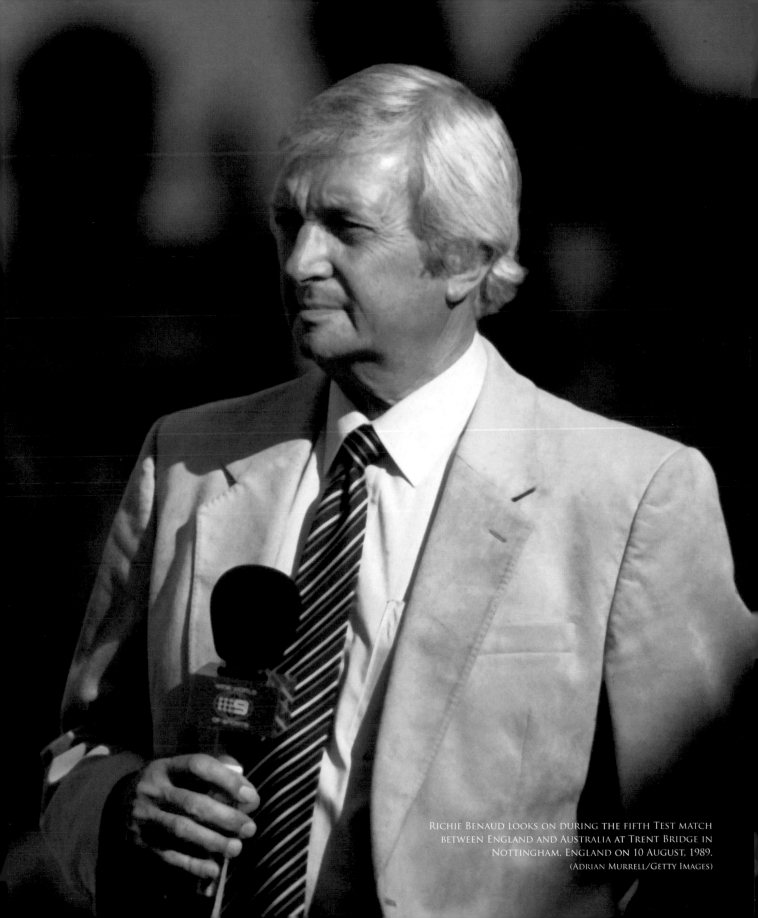

RICHIE BENAUD LOOKS ON DURING THE FIFTH TEST MATCH
BETWEEN ENGLAND AND AUSTRALIA AT TRENT BRIDGE IN
NOTTINGHAM, ENGLAND ON 10 AUGUST, 1989.
(ADRIAN MURRELL/GETTY IMAGES)

CHANNEL 4 COMMENTATOR, RICHIE BENAUD, AT OLD TRAFFORD CRICKET GROUND DURING THE THIRD TEST MATCH BETWEEN ENGLAND AND THE WEST INDIES ON 13 AUGUST 2004 IN MANCHESTER, ENGLAND. (TOM SHAW/ GETTY IMAGES)

Richie was part of the first generation who grew up with cricket on the radio. The ABC started their synthetic broadcasts of Test matches from England in 1934. At Jugiong the 1936–37 Ashes series was heard through 2CO Corowa. The Benaud family's big Kriesler radio was always tuned in. When Bradman took the Australian team to England in 1938, shortwave broadcasts beamed the commentary live from England for the first time. It was the beginning of a ritual that inspired the Test cricketers of future generations; young boys drifting off to sleep listening to their crystal sets, dreaming that they might one day play for Australia.

— STEVE CANNANE FROM *FIRST TESTS: GREAT AUSTRALIAN CRICKETERS AND THE BACKYARDS THAT MADE THEM*

ASHES GO TO SKY

Benaud, recently voted the best cricket commentator ever, will make his final appearance behind the microphone in this country [England] during next week's fifth Test at The Oval. His retirement from the airwaves here is because Test cricket will move from Channel 4 to Sky Sports next summer, depriving terrestrial audiences of seeing a 'new era' of English cricket.

Benaud believes the game's powerbrokers have dropped a major clanger by asking the Government to take home Tests off the 'restricted' list, which prevents rights for certain major events from going to satellite channels.

Benaud will continue to do media work overseas and his absence from the UK airwaves can be seen as a clear indication of his displeasure at the switch to Sky.

The 74-year-old said: 'There are only two groups of people who have control over that. The first is the government of the day and the second is the English Cricket Board.

'It's the ECB who persuaded the Government to take cricket off the restricted list. There is no point asking anyone except the ECB and the Government … .'

— Daily Mirror, 2 September 2005

Fittingly, his real farewell was in England, the place where he first started commentating. It was during the 2005 Ashes series, perhaps the finest ever. Always the democrat, Benaud was standing down in quiet objection to cricket's disappearance from free-to-air television.

'We've had all sorts of music here today,' he started. '*Land of Hope and Glory*, the national anthem – *Jerusalem* before we started. I always carry a lot of music around with me and one of the great ones for me is Andrea Bocelli and Sarah Brightman, singing that duet, that wonderful duet, *Time To Say Goodbye*. And that's what it is as far as I'm concerned – time to say goodbye. And you can add to that – thank you for having me. It's been absolutely marvellous. For 42 years I've loved every moment of it. And it's been a privilege to go into everyone's living room throughout that time. What's even better is that it's been a great deal of fun.'

At that point Kevin Pietersen was bowled by Glenn McGrath, and Richie incorporated it effortlessly. 'But it's not fun for the batsman …' before introducing his fellow commentators.

— Richard Crooke, from *Richie Benaud: A Personal Reflection on a Colossus of Cricket*

GIDEON HAIGH

from *Cricket: The Ashes*

When he seemed set to fade away following Channel 4's capture of cricket broadcast rights in 1999, allies ranging from Piers Morgan to Mick Jagger came together to protest that summer without Richie was unthinkable.

When Channel 4 won the [broadcast] rights, one way they publicly pledged to 'revolutionise' cricket coverage was by banning 'grey-haired old fogeys'. Benaud wrote in his *News of the World* column:

'I see that Channel 4 are not going to have any grey-haired old Fogeys in the com box. I'm sure David Gower and Tony Lewis can look after themselves in this regard but who else could they possibly have in mind?'

A few months later Benaud was having dinner in Canberra with his brother John when the phone rang: it was Channel 4, which had realised that even revolutions need some semblance of continuity.

[But now] it is Benaud, too, who has made the call about his commentary future, by deciding that he is a 'free-to-air man', and thus, although he will continue to work for Kerry Packer's Channel Nine in Australia, he will not be drawn into the new world of Sky. The designation 'free-to-air man' is one he cannot really explain. He believes that 'the differences would be considerable' in working for pay-TV but cannot be specific and finally concludes: 'Let's just say that at 74 I'm in the mindset that, having been free-to-air, I want to stay free-to-air.'

This time [at his retirement from commentating in England] there has been little fuss, no public campaign, no call for a private member's bill to ensure Benaud's preservation in the commentary box a la Jeremy Bentham. Perhaps after the Oval Test, 'morning everyone' will be replaced by mourning everyone, but this summer cricket has taken precedence. There is no doubt that Benaud prefers it this way.

CHANNEL 4 COMMENTATOR, RICHIE BENAUD,
LOOKS ON DURING DAY FOUR OF THE FIFTH ASHES
TEST MATCH BETWEEN ENGLAND AND AUSTRALIA
AT THE OVAL ON 11 SEPTEMBER 2005 IN LONDON,
ENGLAND. (TOM SHAW/GETTY IMAGES)

MIKE ATHERTON

from *Six Laws of Richie*

One of my early broadcasts was from Lord's and, before the start of play, the cameras were to alight on each of the commentators in various parts of the ground, from where they were to analyse a particular aspect of the day's play. We were to come to Richie last of all, up in his eyrie of the commentary box, and he was to be the scene-setter for the day — the last voice to be heard before live play.

I had finished my bit down below and hurried up to the commentary box to listen to the great man do his bit – to watch and learn as instructed. I stood behind the camera at the back of the box and waited. Richie's turn came; on the director's cue, he turned to the camera, with that one-eye-half-closed look, and began to speak. Maybe he thought he had a lapel microphone attached to his (beige/cream/off-white/bone) jacket. He did not. Richie spoke, but the viewers heard nothing.

Franses stood behind the camera, frantically waving and pointing to the hand-held microphone on the desk and instructing Richie to pick it up. Without moving his stare from the camera (Ed Miliband should know that only Richie can do that stare) he felt around blindly on the desk, picked up what he thought was the microphone, lifted to his mouth, and began talking into his glasses.

He didn't miss a beat and later laughed the mistake off and was happy to be the butt of everyone's humour. Therein, I suppose, lies Richie's first Law of broadcasting: 'It's live telly, mistakes happen'. It's also sport on telly and not the most important thing in the world, so don't get too hung up about it and don't imagine yourself to be more important than you really are. You are only a television commentator.

That links in to his second Law – these laws by the way were not written on stone (or tablet these days, I guess) but rather as I imagined them to be, having worked with and watched him for four years and listened to his advice – which is, as he said to me once, 'remember, above all, that you are a guest in someone's living room, often for six hours a day, so try not to irritate them'.

Not irritating the viewer may sound like a limited ambition for a commentator but – as countless viewers of live sport would attest, no doubt – it is not as straightforward as it sounds, especially in cricket where a game might progress for five days for six hours a day. Ideally, you don't want the viewer switching off, or over, or turning the sound down. So remember, above all, that he/she is there to watch the action and the cricketers and not listen to you. Don't impose yourself too heavy-handedly between the viewer and the action. You are a conduit – no more, no less.

If you can succeed in that, Richie may allow you to progress to his third Law which is: 'If you can add to the picture, do so'. Aside from not irritating the viewer into switching off, you are there to add some insight and to inform, based on your knowledge and experience. That insight may be in the form of an anecdote or technical or tactical or human observation, and may be more suitable when the action is slow rather than dramatic, according to your discretion. But anyone can read the score and tell the viewer what has just happened. It's not radio.

Richie's third Law links into his fourth: 'Michael, always engage brain before speaking'. I can't remember what particularly dumb bit of commentary of mine had prompted that from Richie, but it is good advice nonetheless. Radio demands immediacy, since, obviously, people cannot see what is happening. Television occasionally – not always, but occasionally – allows for a momentary distance from the action, just enough time for the brain to function. Use it.

Richie's fifth Law – 'nobody ever complained about silence' – is an old-fashioned notion these days, as increasingly television companies move to three commentators in action rather than two, and so there is a battle for air-time. It also might not apply to an Indian audience who, I am told, enjoy a full-on visual and audio experience – one reason perhaps why Bill Lawry, say, was always more popular on the sub-continent than Richie. Richie has always been immensely popular in England where, I think, audiences enjoyed his understated style, pauses and silences.

And finally: 'Never use the term "We" when talking about a team'. Neutrality and fairness was a non-negotiable for two very good reasons: first, you are an observer not a cheerleader; second, although there will be a home audience, within that there may be many people cheering for the other team. You need to be fair to both sides. Most broadcasts these days go around the world in any case, and so you are speaking to cricket-lovers of all nationalities.

He saw television commentary as a craft, and one to try to excel at. So, in meetings before the start of a Test series, he was meticulous about the pronunciation of names, especially so if, for example, Sri Lanka were touring. And I have lost count of the number of times he said to me: 'It's a pitch, Michael, not a wicket. The three bits of wood are wickets'. Or, 'please don't start interview questions with 'must'.' ('You must be pleased with etc etc' being a statement and not a question.) Small things, but important nonetheless.

He was loved. For longer than people care to remember he was the voice of the English summer, just as he was in Australia. Thinking now, I can hear him, at the culmination of the greatest Test match I have seen at Edgbaston in 2005, exactly the right man for the moment, as he followed the pictures with succinct but dramatic precision: 'Jones! Bowden! Kasprowicz the man to go and Harmison has done it! Despair on the faces of the batsmen and joy for every England player on the field!' Benaud's Laws distilled.

During the afternoon, Michael Slater was on air and was all of a muddle. He wanted to use the past tense of the word 'sneak' but wasn't sure whether it should be snuck or sneaked. He turned to Richie who was eating a sandwich and studying the form. 'Hey Rich,' he whispered, 'can I use the word snuck or is it sneaked? Whaddaya think?' Richie finished his sandwich and ticked his fancy. Then in characteristic fashion he raised an eyebrow and half turned to Slater. 'Michael,' he said, 'quite a few ucks spring to mind, but sn is not one of them.'

— MIKE ATHERTON IN OPENING UP

THE CROWD APPLAUD RICHIE BENAUD AS HE COVERS HIS LAST MATCH ON ENGLISH SOIL DURING DAY FIVE OF THE FIFTH ASHES TEST MATCH BETWEEN ENGLAND AND AUSTRALIA AT THE OVAL ON 12 SEPTEMBER 2005 IN LONDON, ENGLAND. (TOM SHAW/GETTY IMAGES)

GREG CHAPPELL

He was always supportive of me – other than the infamous day at the MCG when I ordered my younger brother Trevor to bowl underarm against New Zealand. His summation of the day was scathing. I was stung by his criticism, because it came from my boyhood hero.

He was, of course, entitled to his opinion and, without the knowledge of some of the things going on in the background, he was entirely correct to be affronted by what I did. I made a mistake for which I have expressed my remorse. It is a decision that I wish I had never made. We never discussed the incident. I didn't feel the need to and I had no doubt that Richie had said what he felt and moved on.

Our relationship was largely unaffected in the aftermath. He continued to be unfailingly generous and gracious in his assessment of me and my career. Though hurt then, I have never held his comments against him. He was not only professional but extremely supportive, when we worked together in the Channel Nine commentary box. The Channel Nine commentary team became iconic in the years that Richie led the band of Test match captains – all of whom held him in the highest esteem.

Amazingly, it was Billy Birmingham, the satirist, with his 12th Man series of parodies of the commentary team who took them to an even wider audience. Birmingham really 'caught' the personalities of Benaud, Lawry and Greig and indeed the commentary box, in a way that endeared them universally. It seemed everyone was practising Richie's 'what a catch' Bill's 'He's got 'im' or Greigy's comments about the 'cor pork and the putch report'!

Some of us in the commentary box, too, would practise our Birmingham Benaud-isms, but not when Richie was around! Bill Lawry is the only one that I saw, who dared to do it to Richie's face and that happened when they were on air together during a domestic one-day game in Hobart in the '90s.

South Australia was playing Tasmania and reached a score of 2–222 which Bill mischievously read as 'chew for chew hundred and chwenty chew' including the pouting bottom lip. Bill thought it was so hilarious that he put the microphone in his lap and collapsed in paroxysms of laughter. Richie probably saw the funny side of it, but he wasn't going to give Bill the pleasure, by joining in the mirth, so he put his microphone in his lap and stared down his nose at Bill and silently dared him to go on.

Each time Bill picked up the microphone he collapsed into laughter and couldn't speak. Richie wouldn't commentate either, so two overs went by without a word while Bill composed himself. Once again, Richie showed his dry wit and sense of timing as he had the last laugh, letting Bill stew in the juice of his own making.

Having learnt his commentary on BBC TV, Richie was economic with words and sharp in his observations. A few generations of commentators have learnt from watching the Master at work. He was the voice of the summer in two countries for many years, as he followed the sun from Australia to England, and, back again.

He led a very full and interesting life, with cricket as the backdrop for most of it. He enriched the game with his love and his knowledge and graced it by never looking backwards and lamenting the past or the changes. He always looked for the positives in the game, and in those who played it.

BILL LAWRY AND RICHIE BENAUD IN THE COMMENTARY BOX
AT ADELAIDE OVAL. (DAVID MARIUZ/NEWSPIX)

MORNING R
MORNING E

Cricket fans hold a Richie Benaud banner during day
four of the fifth Ashes Test match in London, 2005.
(Tom Shaw/Getty Image)

ROBERT MACKLIN

from *Calling the Shots: Beloved cricket commentators*

Every year they arrive like relatives. They burst upon the scene and you're absolutely overjoyed to see them … 'You little beauty!' you cry. 'Hi ya Richie, G'day Tony and Bill and Ian and oh, I see you've brought Greg with you … and little Sunny's there hiding behind Tony's legs. Hi, Sunny. Boy oh boy, this is gonna be terrific.'.

Yes, it's the cricket commentators, those members of a special breed with whom we spend more time in one-sided conversation through the year than any bona fide relative in either the nuclear or the extended family. And television being the searchlight of the soul, we probably get to know them, their strengths and weaknesses, their foibles and prejudices – and on occasion their desperately annoying little habits – better than most of the sprigs on the family kurrajong.

So, what sort of a crew are we dealing with and how have they affected our appreciation of the sport they comment upon? It must be said that their knowledge of and passion for the game are almost 'boundless'. This applies equally to the ABC radio men as to the Nine Network team.

They are pretty forthright in their attitudes and opinions though they have all developed a rather mealy-mouthed formula for expressing their views on a player's performance.

For example, if at a crucial time of the match Azharuddin closes his eyes and essays a barnyard swipe at a McDermott delivery, gets a nick to Healy and thus precipitates a total collapse of the Indian innings, they won't say, 'What a mug. That was about the most idiotic, irresponsible piece of captaincy I've seen since Ray Illingworth… etc.' Not at all. They'll say, 'Azhar will be desperately disappointed with his performance today'.

Or if Merv Hughes bowls three no-balls, two wides and drops a catch in his first over they won't say, 'Merv's been on the turps again. AB should give him a kick in the bum'. Not at all. They'll say, 'Mervyn will not be happy with that'. I'm sure you've noticed it. A little more forthrightness would not go astray.

They have also induced a similar verbal contortion among the players they interview. I suspect this started with David Gower or perhaps Mike Gatting but it's now spread throughout the sporting community. When asked an opinion on just about anything, from the state of the weather to their record five ducks in a row, they'll begin a reply with, 'Well, obviously …' before saying something blindingly obvious like, '… there are formations in the sky which some people suggest are in fact clouds…' or they'll follow the commentators' lead with, '… it is true that my performance in terms of ducks is not something I'm altogether happy with'.

Given the professional nature of the game these days and the legendary sensitivities of controlling bodies like the Australian Cricket Board one can understand their being judicious in their remarks but they take it to extremes and the effect on listeners is a mass inward writhe.

So to those most influential fellows on the other side of the microphones. What sort of companions do they make through the long hot summers? Richie Benaud is the doyen of the breed, the captain

of captains, Richie's cricketing brain is as sharp as ever and he's kept himself trim (even if his facial appearance is somewhat amphibian these days) and in fine mental shape for a very demanding task. He's quite unflappable as anchor and can fill 20 seconds or 20 minutes with interesting chat, incisive commentary and endless reruns of the classic catches. His influence on his colleagues is pervasive.

Richie Benaud commemorated his 500th Test as either player or commentator. That's more than 2000 days playing or watching Test cricket, or about five and a half years back to back, and way more than anyone else, be it Swanton or Woodcock or the beloved CMJ. So when someone of that experience says it's the best thing he's ever seen, you better believe it.

That was the amazing thing about him. Richie often thought it was the best thing he'd ever seen. To him the world kept on improving. He was the antidote to all those septuagenarian nostalgists. He never had an in-my-day thought in his body.

He was Mr Magnanimity, finding a smile and something gently encouraging to say about everything, from streaky shots to dodgy commentary. The only time he was stuck for words was when Dermot Reeve showed him his nipple ring.

His 500 Tests were broken down thus: 63 on the field, five off the field when he was still a player; as a commentator 231 in England, 182 in Australia (oddly, he started working in TV here [England] in 1963 but wasn't accommodated in the commentary box back home [Australia] till 1977) and 19 elsewhere. I don't think he ever got over it. With not a hint of self-satisfaction or vanity, he had no idea his 500th Test was approaching until someone told him. Then, the man who still arrived earlier than anyone else to set up his little nest in the corner of the commentary box, with his laptop and his Laws of Cricket and his racing selections, went beavering away to tot it up for himself. His enthusiasm, his energy and his optimism had him closing on 600 by the time he announced his impending retirement in 2009. Quite remarkable that.

— SIMON HUGHES, FROM *AND GOD CREATED CRICKET*

BATTLE FOR BENAUD

Former Australian cricket captain Richie Benaud has revealed he is battling skin cancer and is undergoing radiation therapy. The highly regarded commentator made his illness public on Monday at the Nine Network's launch for its summer cricket coverage.

Benaud, 84, is receiving treatment for skin cancers on his forehead and the top of his head. 'I'm coping with it very well – the doctors are pleased,' Benaud said at the SCG. 'I'm going along slowly. The cancers need to be treated.'

Benaud urged people to take precautions to protect themselves in the sun. 'I recommend to everyone they wear protection on their heads. Eighty-four-year olds don't seem to mend as well as they used to. When I was a kid, we never ever wore a cap. I wish I had. You live and learn as you go along.'

— AAP, 10 NOVEMBER 2014

TONY GREIG, MARK TAYLOR, RICHIE BENAUD, IAN CHAPPELL AND BILL LAWRY POSE DURING THE CHANNEL NINE 2010–2011 ASHES SERIES LAUNCH AT THE SYDNEY CRICKET GROUND IN NOVEMBER 2010. (MARK NOLAN/GETTY IMAGES

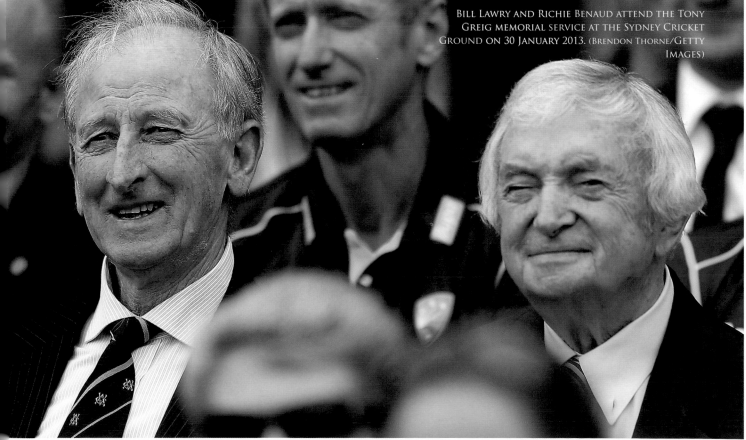

BILL LAWRY AND RICHIE BENAUD ATTEND THE TONY GREIG MEMORIAL SERVICE AT THE SYDNEY CRICKET GROUND ON 30 JANUARY 2013. (BRENDON THORNE/GETTY IMAGES)

The Australian flag is lowered to half mast for Richie Benaud at the Sydney Cricket Ground on 10 April, 2015. (AAP Images)

TRIBUTES

RICHIE BENAUD RINGS THE BELL ON THE PAVILION BALCONY ON THE SECOND DAY OF THE SECOND TEST MATCH BETWEEN ENGLAND AND AUSTRALIA AT LORD'S CRICKET GROUND IN LONDON, 17 JULY, 2009. (AP PHOTO/KIRSTY WIGGLESWORTH/AAP IMAGES)

As a player alone he left a great legacy but as a commentator his gestures and his language were peerless. Wise men often don't inundate you with words but when they speak you listen to everything they say.
— JUSTIN LANGER

Our country has lost a national treasure. After Don Bradman, there has been no Australian player more famous or more influential than Richie Benaud.

Richie stood at the top of the game throughout his rich life, first as a record-breaking leg-spinner and captain, and then as cricket's most famous broadcaster who became the iconic voice of our summer. He was an important influence in the formation of Kerry Packer's World Series Cricket in 1977, a climactic event at the time but one which has left a lasting, positive influence on the game.

Away from the camera he was a leader, mentor and positive influencer of an extraordinary number of cricketers. And despite his role as the treasured grandfather of the game, he remained deeply in touch with modern developments, embracing Twenty20 when others of older eras shunned it. — WALLY EDWARDS, CRICKET AUSTRALIA CHAIRMAN

THOSE SUMMERS OF CRICKET

I grew up with his voice in my ears. On my first trip to Australia he was the man I was most nervous to meet. — GRAEME SMITH

He was one of our own. Always welcome in our living room and the voice of our summer. — MARC HIGGINSON

Richie Benaud epitomised the words of Mark Twain: 'The fear of death follows from the fear of life. A man who lives fully is prepared to die at any time'. Richie led a full and creative life in which fear may have played a very miniscule, inconsequential part.

As a player he prepared well and played with abandon. His captaincy was bold and adventurous and as a broadcaster, he was peerless.

Though, the entire cricketing world held him in the highest esteem and great affection, Richie would not want anyone, to make a fuss of his passing. He will be sorely missed and the game will be much poorer without him.

Vale the Maestro. — GREG CHAPPELL

AT THE LAUNCH OF CHANNEL NINE'S SUMMER OF
INTERNATIONAL CRICKET AT THE SYDNEY CRICKET GROUND,
SYDNEY IN JULY 2006. (AAP-IMAGES)

RICHIE BENAUD STANDS BY A SCULPTURE
OF HIMSELF AT THE SYDNEY CRICKET GROUND
IN JANUARY 2008. (AAP IMAGES)

RICHIE BENAUD, SPORTING A BRUISED EYE, ATTENDS
A SPECIAL REUNION EVENT TO RAISE MONEY FOR THE
MOVEMBER CHARITY IN SYDNEY IN 2010. (AAP IMAGES)

Prime Minister John Howard greets Richie Benaud at the Sydney Cricket Ground. (AAP Images)

RICHIE BENAUD IS INDUCTED INTO THE AUSTRALIAN
CRICKET HALL OF FAME BY IAN CHAPPELL IN 2007.
(GETTY IMAGES)

THANK YOU FOR THE MEMORIES RICHIE BENAUD

A GREAT NEW SOUTH WELSHMAN

A TRIBUTE TO THE LATE RICHIE BENAUD IS SHOWN ON THE BIG SCREEN PRIOR TO A SUPER RUGBY MATCH AT ALLIANZ STADIUM IN SYDNEY. (AAP IMAGES)

RICHIE BENAUD MOMENTS

During a ODI between England and Australia at Edgbaston a stripper ran onto the field only to be grabbed by Rod Marsh and handed over to the officials. Benaud was at his best with the quip,

It's the only thing he's caught all day.

And that's four …
[pauses as ball slows up before the boundary]
… if they can run quickly enough.

Richie's take on Boycott batting all morning:

Slow is one word for it.
Tortuous is another.

Talking about the best piece of advice he'd been given, Tiger O'Reilly told him to develop a really viciously turning leg-break and that it would take him 4 years to do it. He in turn passed the advice on to Shane Warne. Then there was a typical Benaud pause, before he said in his laconic way

He did it in two.

RICHIE BENAUD LEAVES THE GROUND.
(FAIRFAX)

18

RICHIE BENAUD LEAVES THE GROUND.
(FAIRFAX)